Songs
of WAKE FOREST

Tributes by **Edwin G. Wilson**

Edited by Catherine Burroughs and Tamara McLaughlin

WAKE FOREST UNIVERSITY
WINSTON-SALEM, NORTH CAROLINA

Copyright © 2020 Wake Forest University
*All rights reserved, including the right of reproduction,
in whole or in part, in any form.*

ISBN 978-1-61846-113-1

*Design by Urena Design, Winston-Salem, North Carolina.
Manufactured in the United States of America.*

Dedication

In thankful memory

My mother: Annie Saunders Wilson
My father: William Basley Wilson
My brothers: William Laurence Wilson, Thomas Saunders Wilson, Warren Burton Wilson
My sister: Elizabeth Wilson Amos

I heard their "songs" too.

Acknowledgments

The photographs in this book come from a myriad of sources: personal collections, numerous University publications, and multiple collections within the University archives. Within these sources, some images were attributed to specific photographers — whom we wish to thank — while many others were not. Together they represent contributions from Griggs Studio, McNabb Studio, Susan Mullally, and Ken Bennett, along with photos from *The Howler* and *The Wake Forest Magazine*. These images have greatly enhanced our text, and we are grateful to the staff of ZSR Special Collections and Archives, and especially Melde Rutledge, for their work in making them available to us.

Special thanks to Rogan Kersh, Melanie Harkey, Kerry King, Ed Morris, Mika Payden-Travers, and countless others throughout the University who were eager to honor this part of Wake Forest's history and who supported this endeavor in ways big and small.

Last, but certainly not least, we are indebted to Dave Urena, whose thoughtful design and layout choices have brought these stories to life.

Image Citations by Repository

The citations below include the source, followed by the page number on which they appear in this book (in italics), the subject and the photographer if known (in parenthesis).

SPECIAL COLLECTIONS & ARCHIVES (ZSR LIBRARY, WAKE FOREST UNIVERSITY)

History of Wake Forest College Volume IV   *xii* Wait Hall, *22* West, *32* Johnson/Upchurch/Turnage

History of Wake Forest College Volume V   *41* Banks/Venezuela, *43* Casa Artom, *45* Scales Family, *73* B.G & Beena Gokhale, *79* "Doc" Murphrey

The Howler Yearbooks   *1940 Howler: 139* Yearbook Page; *1941 Howler: xii* Corner, *xv* Folk, *xvi* Binkley, *6* Folk/Chaucer, *139* Freshman Badge; *1962 Howler: 8* Folk/colleagues, *40* Banks/artifact, *64* Nowell/colleagues, *101* Bryan; *1963 Howler: 15* Tribble/convention, *15* Tribble/walking; *1965 Howler: 47* Reece/Hill, *50* Dyer/student, *87* Robinson/colleagues; *1966 Howler: 74* Gokhale/students, *132* Williams/lecture; *1968 Howler: 58* Starling; *1969 Howler: 36* Hollingsworth/students, *67* Brantley; *1973 Howler: 42* Scales, *46* Reece, *49* Dyer, *66* Russell & Lib Brantley, *68* Crisp, *72* Gokhale, *80* Gossett, *93* Burroughs, *109* Elmore/student, *122* Preseren/student, *133* Waddill; *1974 Howler: 28* Schoonmaker; *1975 Howler: 56* Starling, *88* Angell/students, *91* Burroughs, *96* Phillips/colleagues, *119* Potter; *1976 Howler: 10* Reinhardt, *38* L. Aycock/colleagues, *59* Shaw, *62* Nowell, *69* Crisp/student, *86* P. Robinson, *120* Preseren; *1977 Howler: 92* Burroughs, *100* Bryan, *110* Elmore, *116* Covey, *119* Potter/student; *1978 Howler: 82* Gossett, *132* Williams; *1979 Howler: 90* Angell, *98* Stroupe; *1980 Howler: 29* Schoonmaker/colleagues, *131* Williams

University Archives Photograph Collection   *xi* Old Well, *xv* Jones (McNabb Studio), *xvi* Memory (Irvin Grigg), *3* Aycock/colleagues, *9* Folk/Jones/students, *13* Tribble, *14* Tribble/student (Grigg Studio), *16* Luther (Susan Mullally Clark), *21* West (McNabb Studio), *25* Easley (Susan Mullally Clark), *26* Allen & Madge Easley (McNabb Studio), *31* Johnson (Grigg Studio), *37* L.Aycock/M.Brown (Susan Mullally Clark), *39* Banks (Susan Mullally Clark), *40* Banks/students (Susan Mullally Clark), *54-55* McPherson (Susan Mullally Clark), *60* Shaw/student (Stan Carmical), *65* Brantley (Susan Mullally Clark), *75-76* Allen (Susan Mullally Clark), *84* Davis/Casa Artom (Susan Mullally Clark), *85* Davis/trustees (Susan Mullally Clark), *95* Phillips (Susan Mullally Clark), *103* Beck, *104-105* Mandelbaum/students (Susan Mullally Clark), *107* Robinson (Susan Mullally Clark), *111* Mitchell (Susan Mullally Clark), *112* Mitchell/Easley/Davis (Susan Mullally Clark), *118* Potter, *128* Christman (Susan Mullally Clark), *137* Dodding (Susan Mullally Clark)

University and N.C. Baptist Biographical Files Collections   *2* Aycock, *18-20* Hayes, *24* Easley/Scales, *35* Hollingsworth

Wake Forest Magazine   *December 1957: xv* Reid; *February 1964: 83* Davis, Jr.; *March 1973: 32* Johnson; *November 1970: 11* Reinhardt/Evans

Wake Forest Original Campus Collection   *xi* Snyder, *xiv* Poteat, *xvii* Lois & Gerald Johnson, *7* Folk

WAKE FOREST PHOTO ARCHIVE

xiii Shorty's (Ken Bennett), *70* El-Beshti (Ken Bennett), *102* Beck (Ken Bennett), *117* Covey (Ken Bennett), *123* Maya Angelou, *124* Angelou/students (Ken Bennett), *124* Angelou Hall (Lauren Olinger, Red Cardinal Studio), *127* Ed & Jean Christman (Ken Bennett), *129* Christman/Medallion, *129* Christman/chapel (Ken Bennett), *135* Clara & Charles Allen (Ken Bennett), *137* Wolfe & Tedford (Ken Bennett), *143* Seal (Ken Bennett)

PERSONAL & FAMILY COLLECTIONS

Speas Family: 33 Iona Speas; *Emily Wilson: 51* Ammons (Susan Mullally Clark); *Melanie Harkey: 108* Robinson/students; *Doug Maynard: 113* M. Maynard, *114* Doug & Mary Anne Maynard (Grigg Studio); *Niven Family: 125* Penelope Niven; *Johnson Family: 130* Eunice Johnson

Preface
by Tamara McLaughlin ix

Introduction
The Heritage of Wake Forest   xi   30 March 1996

Tributes

Andrew Lewis Aycock	2	12 April 1978
Edgar Estes Folk	6	3 January 1982
Jon Reinhardt	10	26 May 1984
Harold W. Tribble	13	19 June 1986
K.A.N. Luther	16	22 January 1988
Harold Hayes	18	18 April 1989
Carlton Prince West	21	20 June 1991
Allen Easley	24	6 July 1992
Don Schoonmaker	28	23 May 1993
Lois Johnson	31	23 October 1993
Iona Wells Speas	33	27 August 1994
L. H. Hollingsworth	35	27 February 1995
Lucile Aycock	37	17 June 1995
Pendleton Banks	39	18 August 1995
James Ralph Scales	42	18 March 1996
Mark Reece	46	15 May 1997
Bob Dyer	49	17 April 2001
Archie Ammons	51	19 April 2001
Dolly McPherson	54	11 May 2001
Bill Starling	56	22 June 2001
Bynum Shaw	59	30 August 2001
Jack Nowell	62	20 November 2001
Russell Brantley	65	16 February 2005
Marjorie Crisp	68	16 February 2005
Bashir El-Beshti	70	24 March 2005
B. G. Gokhale	72	16 August 2005
Charles Allen	75	3 September 2005
Willis Everette "Doc" Murphrey	78	9 December 2005
Thomas F. Gossett	80	15 December 2005
Egbert Davis, Jr.	83	12 November 2006

Tributes

Paul Robinson	86	4 March 2007
Bill Angell	88	14 September 2007
Julian Burroughs	91	12 May 2008
Elizabeth Phillips	95	3 September 2008
Henry Stroupe	98	25 August 2009
McLeod Bryan	100	3 Ocotber 2010
Robert Beck	102	10 September 2011
Allen Mandelbaum	104	13 October 2012
Mary Frances Robinson	107	2 September 2012
Tom Elmore	109	2 November 2012
Carlton Mitchell	111	16 February 2013
Mary Anne Maynard	113	26 October 2013
Cyclone Covey	116	1 December 2013
Lee Potter	118	28 January 2014
Herman Preseren	120	17 May 2014
Maya Angelou	123	7 June 2014
Penelope Niven	125	8 September 2014
Ed Christman	127	30 December 2014
Eunice Johnson	130	11 June 2015
Jack Williams	131	12 November 2015
Marcellus Waddill	133	27 August 2016
Clara Allen	135	9 September 2017
Don Wolfe	137	27 April 2019
The Essence of Wake Forest	139	15 July 2010

Afterword
by Catherine Burroughs   147

About the Author   149

About the Editors   150

Preface

Ed Wilson's relationship with Wake Forest began when he entered the College as a freshman in 1939 and has continued for more than eight decades. He has been a teacher, administrator, colleague, mentor and friend to countless Wake Foresters. Throughout his tenure, he has paid tribute to many in the Wake Forest family whose lives have intersected with his – sometimes speaking on behalf of the University and other times as a personal friend of the family. Some of the remembrances here were traditional eulogies given at funerals. Others were a few words shared in small gatherings. Still others were remarks offered at retirement or memorial celebrations.

Regardless of the setting, the depth of his relationship with the individual, or the length of the remarks, a common refrain echoes throughout these pages. Each song is different, each contribution unique, but the refrain is clear – gratitude for those who not only shared their professional talents but their personal passions as well. He offers praise for individuals who came to teach one subject, but whose personal interests contributed to the addition of new departments, the construction of new spaces, and who were responsible for countless "firsts" – Wake Forest's first research conference, semester abroad, museum … the list goes on. These tributes are the songs of men and women who shaped both the content and the character of the University as we know it today. They are full of warmth, humor and, of course, poetry.

The remembrances collected here are book-ended by two of Dr. Wilson's speeches. We open with "The Heritage of Wake Forest," offering a glimpse into life on the Old Campus and its founding values of discipline and passion, friendship and imagination, wisdom, hope, and faith – themes repeated throughout the remembrances. We close with "The Essence of Wake Forest," a variation on the theme, calling Wake Foresters to carry forward this legacy – a legacy marked by friendship and honor, learning and Pro Humanitate.

Whether you know the particular individuals spoken of here or not, our hope is that you will recognize parts of your own song within these remembrances and that they will bring to mind other Wake Foresters whose names do not appear in these pages, but whose songs resonate with these same ideals.

Tamara McLaughlin

The Heritage of Wake Forest

AFTER ALMOST FORTY YEARS THE MEMORY HAS NOT FADED. I walk across this beautiful campus and into this wonderful and so friendly town, and once again I am sixteen, seventeen, eighteen, nineteen, twenty years old, full of hope and expectation, rejoicing in the day and in the company of colorful and faithful friends. Everywhere I look, my imagination stirs.

There, by the Old Well, in the twilight hours of a spring evening, I lie on the grass, listening to the sounds of a Beethoven Symphony coming from an upper room of Wait Hall, where Thane McDonald has placed on the music department's turntable a set of worn 78 rpm records. Never again will Beethoven seem more alive or more powerful.

The Old Well

Over yonder in the Social Science Building, in the hall outside the College Book Store, three or four students gather to watch Connecticut Yankee John Conley serve a ping pong ball to an already defeated opponent, giving with his paddle such a twist to the ball that every time, seemingly, the ball hits the very rim of the opposite side of the table. Around the corner, inside the store, Everette Snyder or one of the Cole brothers serves up a "black cow," and I wander to a rack of newly created PocketBooks, where James Hilton's *Lost Horizon* and Pearl Buck's *Good Earth* are available for twenty-five cents apiece. At a nearby table four Lambda Chis get ready for yet another hand of bridge.

Everette Snyder serves customers at the soda shop in the College Book Store.

In the rotunda of Wait Hall, a place of unexpected grace and beauty, Thurman Kitchin or D.B. Bryan or Elliott Earnshaw or Grady Patterson looks out from his office to say hello. These are all quiet and gentle men who seem not to have heard of pomp and circumstance. They speak, in an unhurried way, of enrollments and budgets – and, maybe, golf. Edith Earnshaw, one of the gallant Taylor sisters, comes out of the Bursar's office, bringing to the group of men a welcome touch of poetry.

Wait Hall

On the "bumming" corner by Miss Jo's, I take my place among the students waiting for a ride to Raleigh. Maybe I am tenth or fifteenth in line, but I know that eventually a car will stop. We are, after all, on U.S. Highway No.1, and the traffic is steady. It is beginning to snow.

The "bumming" corner

I am going to the State Theatre in Raleigh for the Wake County premiere of *Gone with the Wind* and, afterwards, I will have Chinese food at the Canton Restaurant on Hillsborough Street.

Across the street from the place where Faculty Avenue meets the rock wall on the north side of the campus is a brick building where Mrs. Newsome's boarding house staff serves meat, vegetables, desserts, and iced tea – all of excellent quality – to a dining room full of students. Music is being played while we wait for the meal: "Moonlight Serenade," "Star Dust," "I'm Getting Sentimental Over You," "In the Mood," "My Prayer is to linger with you / at the end of the day / in a dream that's divine." The songs all speak wistfully of romantic love on this all-male campus, and we look ahead to that rare weekend in Raleigh or Durham when, for a change, we will not be alone.

The first home football game of the season is about to begin, and I join hundreds of students coming out of Bostwick and Hunter to make their way past the Gymnasium down the little street that leads toward Gore Field. Even by the standards of 1939, the setting is not impressive – seats built into the sides of a hill, no amenities, no hot-dogs, not even (I think) an announcer – but the spirit is contagious and cleansing, and Wake Forest wins. By chance I walk home with Phil Utley, my physical education teacher, who will later that year try – in vain – to show me how to use the parallel bars.

Every day I go to the Post Office, down the steps that cross the railroad tracks, past Mr. Brewer's store, and into the center of town. If I am hungry, I stop – out of deeply engrained habit – at Shorty's for a nickel hamburger. I take a look at the posters in front of the Collegiate Theatre, cross the street to look at what's happening at the Forest Theatre, stop at the College Soda Shop to say hello to Fred or Ben or "Smut," and at the post office (in later years) am greeted from the service window by Lib Greason, who apparently knows us all. On the way back, I may get a haircut from Barney Powell, buy a tube of toothpaste from Tom Holding, cash a check at Mr. Satterwhite's bank, or linger at Hardwicke's Drug Store to watch a train go by. Beyond the tracks appears the arch, gateway to the campus, a familiar invitation to learning.

A group of Wake Foresters visit the original Shorty's for lunch.

On one of those Sundays when I wake up in time, I attend services at the Baptist Church. The speaker is Everett Gill, a returned missionary from Eastern Europe. His text is the parable of the Good Samaritan, and he likens the man who fell among thieves to the many Europeans now being killed by the Nazis. America should be the Good Samaritan, he says. It is a role we are not yet ready for, but when December 7, 1941, arrives, and Bob Lide comes running up the steps at Mrs. Richard Brewer's house to tell us about the attack at Pearl Harbor, we understand what Dr. Gill had meant. A year later, on another December day, I go to Raleigh – this time on a bus, for I wish to remain neatly dressed – to join the Naval Reserve. My last term as a Wake Forest undergraduate is about to begin.

The British essayist G.K. Chesterton once said that half of education is "atmosphere." Well, we at Wake Forest had "atmosphere," and it enveloped the whole community – created not out of wealth or possessions or social standing but out of simple trust, good will, camaraderie, and a sense of belonging. At our best we reached not outward for what the world might give us but inward for what we might find within ourselves to give the world. In this place, comforting and challenging, we absorbed – almost, as it were, from the air – both friendship and purpose.

If half of education comes from the atmosphere and from what students learn by themselves and from one another, the other half comes from teachers. In my freshman year at Wake Forest I read an essay by Gerald W. Johnson in *The Student* magazine. Borrowing his title from the playwright Luigi Pirandello, he called it "Six Characters in Search of an Author." His subject was six professors from his own student days: James W. Lynch, Benjamin Sledd, N.Y. Gulley, Willis Cullom, J.H. Gorrell, and William Louis Poteat. They made Wake Forest, Gerald Johnson said, "a place of gracious memories."

Today, with apologies to Mr. Johnson, I choose also to remember "six characters in search of an author." I will necessarily overlook all those under whom I did not study: Bradbury and Cocke; Black and Isbell; "Math" Jones and Raynor; Parcell, Aycock, Earp, Paschal, and Easley. And I will not include the young men who were in my years (1939–1943) just beginning their long Wake Forest careers: Charles Allen and Percival Perry and Henry Stroupe and Robert Helm and Justus Drake and D.A. Brown. Also, because time is limited, I can do no more than mention the sly and provocative C.C. "Skinny" Pearson, as brilliant a teacher as I have ever known; Carlton West, whose lectures were models of intellectual precision; Bill Speas, whose physics classes were displays of scientific and comic delight; Forrest Clonts, who brought to his history courses a worldly wisdom and a mischievous humor not often found at Wake Forest; Grover Carroll and Roland Gay, who taught mathematics so kindly and so clearly that even English majors felt comfortable in their classrooms.

Inevitably, I suppose, I begin with Hubert McNeill Poteat, not because I would declare him the very best teacher but because he bestrode the campus like a Colossus, and he was always exhilarating. Everything he did he did on a grand scale. When he gave a recital on the church organ, he played Wagner preludes and the William Tell Overture – not, as he said in class one day, some "namby-pamby, twinkling" music. When he presented a public reading, he chose Marc Connelly's *Green Pastures* and delighted in playing DeLawd (God) – "typecasting," some of us said. He played tennis with vigor; he wore on ceremonial occasions – in the manner of the Imperial Potentate that he was – the colorful costume of a Shriner; in the middle of class he would open a window to shout hello to a passing colleague or sniff the air to see whether the state legislature over in Raleigh was in session that day. His subject was Latin, but what he gave us was passion.

Hubert McNeill Poteat

A.C. Reid was different from Hubert Poteat. Dignified, perfectly groomed, unruffled by circumstance, he taught us "manners" and "virtue." His classroom in Wait Hall was famously a place of control. The door was closed firmly when class began; there was no trash on

A.C. Reid

the floor, there were no knife carvings on the desks; from the students, no slumping in seats or chewing of gum or nodding asleep. I always thought that Dr. Reid was secretly amused by his reputation for order; in his office he would relax, smoke a pipe, smile, and talk easily and naturally. When I last saw him, he was ninety-three years old, he was in a hospital bed, and both his legs had been amputated. But his intellect was clear, his questions were probing, and he smiled when he said good-bye. Dr. Reid's subject was

philosophy, but what he gave us was discipline.

Broadus Jones, like Dr. Reid, was calm and assured, but he showed us even less of the man beneath the surface. He was expert at playing parts: reading a humorous essay on "noses," becoming Scrooge and all the Ghosts in a holiday performance of Dickens' "Christmas Carol," speaking to a Rotary Club, giving a chapel talk on the universe of John Milton. And I remember one morning in a Shakespeare class when all of a sudden, I heard him reading Hamlet's "To be or not to be" soliloquy – not from the printed page but from the interior of his own private self – and the classroom air became filled with longing and sadness and mystery. Dr. Jones appeared always to know more than he chose to tell us, and he seemed quietly amused at

Broadus Jones

the disparity. Something was there, he knew, which could not be spoken or ever understood. Dr. Jones's subject was English, but what he gave us was imagination.

Edgar Folk was Dr. Jones's departmental colleague, and he was

Edgar Folk

the favored mentor of those students who wanted to learn how "to write." He had been a newspaperman himself, and he could tell us from his own experience about New York City life in the 1920's, when John Barrymore was on the stage and every now and then there was a new play by Eugene O'Neill. He taught Chaucer, and we traveled with him and other pilgrims down the fabled road to Canterbury, but I was especially grateful for the way he brought the love of literature into our own times. In his class on the modern novel we read Hemingway and Steinbeck,

James Joyce and D.H. Lawrence, Edith Wharton and Virginia Woolf: a startling menu for a Southern Baptist college in 1942. Dr. Folk was easy to be with – available and unthreatening – and, for those of us who worked on publications, always "around." He even went with us once to Josh Turnage's for barbecue, and many nights – hat on his head, pipe in his mouth – he sat with us in the *Old Gold and Black* office, helping us with stories and headlines. Dr. Folk's subject was English, but what he gave us was friendship.

Jasper Memory was the featured speaker for my first year orientation, and we freshmen knew at once that this was a man who loved Wake Forest – deeply and without reservation. His eyes would light up with excitement as he told us about Wake Forest alumni who had done well – one of them, a New York lawyer, who had come back to the campus in a car as long as a telephone pole. Professor Memory was a man's man with a full and resounding voice, and his heart sometimes overruled his mind, but his heart was big and his enthusiasms were genuine. Not surprisingly, he liked to sing, and I remember going with him and Thane McDonald and Thompson Greenwood to an alumni meeting in the Conway (North Carolina) Baptist Church, where the four of us sang, "Give me some men who are stouthearted men who will fight for the right they adore." Jasper Memory was a stout-hearted man – never more so than during those many years when he lovingly tended his ill wife, Margaret. I never knew him not to be cheerful. His subject was education, but what he gave us was hope.

Jasper Memory

The sixth professor is Olin T. Binkley. He still lives in Wake Forest, and he is with us today, and we are in his chapel. (I am grateful that I can acknowledge him publicly.) Dr. Binkley, of course, would not remember it, but he gave me the first compliment I ever received as a Wake Forest student. On the first paper he returned to me, he wrote, "Your work pleases me – O.T.B." The words were restrained and cautious, but I treasure them beyond other words because they came from a man of uprightness and honesty such as I have seldom known.

Olin T. Binkley

From my still preserved notes taken in his courses on the life and teachings of Jesus and the life and teachings of Paul, I could almost reconstruct his meticulously planned and meticulously delivered lectures, but I could never recapture satisfactorily what I took to be the essence of his classes: that we were urged to be free to read without boundaries and to explore and to raise questions and to wander far afield but that we could still come back safely to the living words of Scripture. It is possible, he showed us, to be a thoroughly modern scholar and yet at the same time to believe. Dr. Binkley's subject was religion, and what he gave us was faith.

Gerald Johnson, as I have said, spoke of "six characters in search of an author." I have one clear advantage over Mr. Johnson: during my senior year at Wake Forest women were officially admitted to the college, and I experienced one exciting and blissful year of coeducation. Foremost among the newcomers was Gerald Johnson's own sister, Lois Johnson, the first Dean of Women. She stands apart in my memories today as a seventh "character in search of an author."

Lois Johnson with brother Gerald Johnson

Everyone agreed that Lois Johnson was the ideal person to be Dean of Women. Her family credentials were impeccable: she was a vibrant member of the Johnson McNeill-McMillan-Memory clan which had sent so many talented sons to Wake Forest. Now the family had given us a "daughter," comparably talented and even more charming. She was gracious without artifice, kind without sentimentality, intelligent without pretentiousness, and forceful without arrogance. She seemed, somehow, always glad to be alive, and in her presence others were glad to be alive too. Under her guidance women learned to love Wake Forest as men had loved it for more than a century, and the college changed into a better and richer – and more natural – place. Fifty years later, we probably cannot begin to appreciate what a difficult assignment she accepted when she came here, but her good sense and her wit saw her through. She was truly wise. Her job was to be Dean of Women, but what she gave us all, men and women alike, was wisdom.

And so today we celebrate the heritage of Wake Forest: discipline and passion, friendship and imagination, wisdom and hope and faith.

We remember who we were "once upon a time," and we honor those who helped and inspired us. But we do not live in memories. The present – and the future – are still ours, at least for a while. The gift of Wake Forest is not the courses we took or the degrees we received or even the pleasures of these reunion recollections. Nor is the gift of Wake Forest limited to this campus, however hallowed, or to us "old campus" alumni, however loyal. Wake Forest is not a place or a generation. It is an idea, an ideal, and it is to this idea, this ideal, in its transcendence, that we commit ourselves. To remember the Wake Forest that we knew is to remember youth and joy and freedom, and to continue to love Wake Forest is to honor youth and joy and freedom where they most often reside: that is, in the young and the joyful and the free. College is, then and now, for the young. We were young once; others are young now. Together – in union and in friendship – let us with them, today and in the years to come, sing of Wake Forest as we have always sung of Wake Forest:

> *Thine is a noble name;*
> *Thine is a glorious fame,*
> *Constant and true.*
> *We give thee of our praise,*
> *Adore thine ancient days.*
> *Sing thee our humble lays,*
> *Mother, so dear.*

Edwin G. Wilson
March 30, 1996

Tributes

In addition to teaching English, Mr. Aycock taught the first art classes at Wake Forest and was instrumental in the University's addition of an art department.

Andrew Lewis Aycock

Alumnus, English Faculty

ONE OF THE MOST PERVASIVE themes of *Paradise Lost* is the poet Milton's conviction that "service is perfect freedom." Milton was one of Mr. Aycock's favorite poets – from study as well as from natural sympathy with the grand Christian design of the epics – and for years he taught a course in Milton. I do not know whether he stressed in his classrooms the Miltonic-Christian ideal of service; I do know that throughout a lifetime of gentle strength he showed all of us what it means to serve.

Some persons choose a life of service, hoping that it will lead also to rewards: to position, to money, to recognition and acclaim. Mr. Aycock elected to serve others – his family, his friends, his students, his University – because for him there was no alternative: life was service. And so, for more than forty years, he did what is required of faculty members: he taught, he graded papers, he went to meetings: the pattern is familiar and cherished. And generations of Wake Forest students and teachers can tell us how skillful and how imaginative and how versatile he was in all these roles. But he also did those other things that had to be done when no one else admitted having the time or the talent or the desire to do them. How long, for example, was he director of freshman English, that

From left: Professors Aycock, Earp, Cocke & Memory

most burdensome and most vexing of college courses? How many themes must he have read during his career – and yet the 10,000th theme had to have the same attention and respect as the first? How often did we his colleagues come to him with our problems – whether to ask him to repair a ditto machine that our clumsy hands and bookish minds could not master, or to seek counsel on an issue of decisive importance to the college, or of personal concern to ourselves, when there was not much light and we needed an opinion that was fair and wise? And we went to him because we knew that any time we asked him for help, his immediate answer would be "yes" – given not reluctantly but cheerfully.

"Service is perfect freedom": Mr. Aycock served and, because he served, he was free – free from pride, from anger, and from that most crippling of sins, envy. He spent much of his time in out-of-the-way places – on the top floor of the revered Alumni Building on the old campus, in the basement of Tribble Hall, in the slide room of the Fine Arts Center – "mansions" offstage, where he could be (and was) free. He stepped forth quickly to express joy in the success of others, and if applause came to him also, as it often did, that was all right too. But he did not covet what others had – their titles or their honors. I never knew a man in whom there was less meanness or less duplicity.

Mr. Aycock was also free from fear of time and mutability, those ancient foes of man. When the College moved to Winston-Salem, he came with it optimistically and enthusiastically – in middle life, still a pioneer. Because there was a need for art courses, obvious to everyone else but also ignored by everyone else, he began teaching European and American Art – as far as I know, a change in disciplines without precedent at Wake Forest, and yet in keeping with the fortitude of a man who in his sixties was still looking ahead. In him the change from active service to so-called "retirement" was barely noticeable: he was still on the campus, early and late, often doing the work of others when he was weaker and more in need of rest than they. I must speak too of that change from health to sickness that came so suddenly fifteen or sixteen months ago – a change that brought pain and what must have seemed endless days and nights of suffering – and yet this change too he encountered with courage, and, the last time I saw him in January, still with a smile. We recall here, especially, that he was free from grimness and despair. He was a happy man – one of the few men I have known in whom the twinkle of an eye was not just a figure of speech. His eye really did twinkle.

Most of all, because Mr. Aycock was free, he was at peace with himself. He was not divided. In public, in private, at church, in class, abroad or at home, he was the same. His beloved wife Lucile – devoted, resolute, showing that "comfort in the strength of love" that springs only from determination and grace – his two daughters Delia and Jane; his sons-in-law Glenn and Bob; his grandchildren Abner, Laura Lu, Mardee, Sarah Ann; his brother, his sister, they will remember moments of tenderness and affection beyond anything the rest of us can claim. But the difference is in degree only. If I were to ask all those who knew Mr. Aycock what he was like, they would answer in the same way, I believe – whether I approached a student who once came rejoicing to his office with, at last, an A paper in his hand; or another student who, after much patient explaining, finally understood what a comma splice is – or, for that matter, still failed to understand what it is; or a young colleague angry about some slight or some injustice and desperately wanting encouragement; or a co-worker in the slide library frustrated by the constant need to be so careful and meticulous; or an alumnus recalling his years at Wake Forest and eager for a listener to share his memories with; or a building custodian who, at some unexpected hour, cleans the office and finds "that nice man" alone and still at work; or a young high school girl by his side in the museums of Europe, looking up to him as he shows her with words the beauty of the art they see and by his illumined face the beauty of the hours they are spending together. They would all say, I believe, that Mr. Aycock saw them with the intentness of one who cared, that he heard them patiently, that he spoke to them kindly. Without being stern he was righteous, and without being soft he was good.

For me the words of Scripture that come most naturally to mind when I think of Mr. Aycock are that he was "pure in heart." "Blessed are the pure in heart, for they shall see God."

April 12, 1978

Edgar Estes Folk

Alumnus, English/Journalism Faculty
Received the Medallion of Merit in 1974

IN THE 1941 EDITION OF *The Howler*, the Wake Forest College year book, is a photograph of two men in conversation with each other: one, an older man with a short white beard, dressed in medieval costume, is speaking; the other, a modern man in his forties, wearing a neat dark suit and a trim mustache, is listening. On the wall behind the men is a picture adorned with other men on horseback moving toward some common destination.

Wake Forest students in 1941 – indeed, Wake Forest students during any one of the years from 1936 to 1967 – would have had no difficulty in identifying the figures in the photograph. The speaker from the Middle Ages was Geoffrey Chaucer, the peerless author of *Canterbury Tales*; the twentieth-century listener was Edgar Estes Folk, an English professor who, after only five years on the faculty, had already become, in the words of the 1941 *Howler*, "an indispensable part of Wake Forest." The horsemen in the picture were pilgrims on the way to the shrine of Thomas à Becket in Canterbury Cathedral: characters no less dear to Dr. Folk than to Geoffrey Chaucer himself.

The photograph that shows these men of the fourteenth and twentieth centuries talking to each other, though the "trick" work of an ingenious cameraman, is symbolically correct. For Dr. Folk, whose life and acts we celebrate today, was a man who was happy and comfortable in the past: that forever magical April day when "nyne and twenty" Canterbury pilgrims came to the Tabard Inn in Southwark, England; or that February day in 1834 when Samuel Wait and the other "founders" of Wake Forest College met in the Calvin Jones house to give birth to a school of "glorious fame, constant and true"; or some other less widely known day from history when a book he loved was published or a piece of furniture he admired was built.

The story of Wake Forest, both college and town, was to Dr. Folk

more than a twice-told tale – a narrative to be treasured and savored and remembered with joy. His own family had known Wake Forest almost from its beginnings (Henry Bate Folk, his grandfather, was a distinguished member of the class of 1849), and the Folk line has continued without interruption through five generations: a grandson, Thomas Geoffrey Folk, is a college freshman this year. The stately brick house, across the street from this church, where he lived, is a place of elegance as old as Wake Forest itself: a home to which Dr. Folk and his devoted wife Minta Holding Folk brought antiques of rare value and beauty. Every room, every wall, every corner has its own rewards for the eye and the mind. And Dr. Folk's eye and mind saw it all as precious – each door, each table, each book.

But the Dr. Folk that most of us recall so fondly today, though a medievalist and an antiquarian, was also a thoroughly modern man. As a newspaperman on the *New York Herald,* he had observed and recorded the day-to-day life of the city, with all its variety and excitement. And throughout the formative years of the 1920's and 1930's, he had seen plays by dramatists like Eugene O'Neill who were shaping a new American theatre and read books by men like Joyce and Faulkner and Hemingway who were redefining the possibilities of the modern novel. His students at Wake Forest were to become his eager followers through the streets and pages of America; because of him they heard about – and read – *Strange Interlude, A Farewell to Arms, The Grapes of Wrath, An American Tragedy.*

For Dr. Folk, the beloved past and the vibrant present met in the classroom and in those college publications offices where the students who perhaps loved him most gathered to listen, to ask and answer questions, and to write. He was a master teacher. We who were his students know that he was because of our own grateful memories; if we respect words and if we respect the truth, we do so in part because he taught us that they are linked irrevocably. Those among us who were not his students should know that in newspaper offices and college classrooms all over the country there are Wake Forest men and women who came to where they are because something Dr. Folk once said made them write better or think more clearly or act more responsibly.

The secret of Dr. Folk's success as a teacher was not primarily in his

From right: Professors Folk, Wilson and Harris, members of the 1962 Faculty Publications Board who served as advisors for the Old Gold & Black, The Student, *and* The Howler.

learning, considerable though it was, or in the traditional talents of the pedagogue. He seldom lectured, and his courses were not formally organized. His strength lay in his casualness, his ease, the way in which he could hint or suggest, his patience, his very reluctance to assume authority. Most of us, I suspect, remember less than we should of what he said; rather we recall his look, his presence, his humanity – his character. Like Chaucer's knight – I hope Dr. Folk will forgive the modernization – he loved "chivalry, truth and honor, freedom and courtesy."

As I have thought about Dr. Folk these last two days, two images in particular have come to mind. One is of a Wake Forest alumni magazine cover of eleven years ago. It shows Dr. Folk standing at the entrance to the Wake Forest Cemetery, where so many Wake Forest faculty members are buried. Unlike this January day the weather is warm and bright: the trees are green, and the crepe myrtles are in full bloom. Dr. Folk is about to conduct a tour of a place that, in an inside story, he says has "an air of serenity and peace." If the Wake Forest men and women who lie in the cemetery, wrote Dr. Folk, "have been portrayed [by me]... as of heroic mold it is because... the students saw them as such." We "take off our hats and bow our heads in a salute to those who... bequeathed the ideals and memories to make... Wake Forest." They knew, Dr. Folk said, that a Wake Forest "education is not for selfish men."

From left: Professors Folk and Jones with students

The second image is of a pilgrimage coming to an end. Since Chaucer's pilgrims never arrived at Canterbury, I must turn to another English writer, John Bunyan, for the story of one pilgrim who at the end of his "progress" did reach the city of his hopes. "I heard," wrote Bunyan, "that all the bells in the city rang... for joy, and... it was said unto the pilgrim, *Enter ye into the joy of your Lord*... And as the gates to the city were opened to let in the pilgrim, I looked..., and, behold, the City shone like the sun."

January 3, 1982

Jon Reinhardt
Political Science Faculty

Here in this quiet place, on this late May afternoon, on this still campus, five days after the sounds of graduation have passed away, we meet to remember and to honor Jon Reinhardt, whose life came to an end even as the school year came to an end: Jon Reinhardt, husband, father, son, brother, teacher, colleague, friend.

And in remembering and honoring Jon Reinhardt we look for signals from within his life, so well and so richly lived, that will give us a better understanding of who he was and who we are.

Our memories of Jon are vivid and clear. He was a person whose face and features were, always and freshly, alive with meaning. I remember the day, more than twenty years ago, when I first saw him. He was on the campus to be interviewed for the teaching position which he later accepted, and we met in one of the corridors of Reynolda Hall. I liked him at once. He was, of course, a young man – a boy, I would almost have said – and he had that look, those gestures, that we all were to become so familiar with during the good years that followed: eyes that sparkled and danced with unconcealed, almost naive excitement; hands that moved and touched as if to capture in one generous circle both the idea and the listener; a smile that enveloped his surroundings with curiosity and love. I could not have known what a good teacher he would become, but I knew that he would bring vitality and passion to everything he did.

Twenty years of Wake Forest students can speak with appreciation and affection of what happened next. For Jon quickly became one of Wake Forest's memorable teachers, winning just six years later the college's first "excellence in teaching" award.

Some teachers achieve respect by the force of their intellect, and Jon, too, was prepared by study and by intentness of mind to teach with learning and authority. Others become admired because their personality is easy and appealing and invites confidence, and Jon was surely a happy and generous friend to those he taught. But Jon had something more: he gave to his students an extraordinary sense of affirmation.

He was, in the words of one student, "a sort of promise of what can be good and right in men and women." He could grasp the implications of political powers and principalities and remain, nevertheless, enthusiastic, youthful, and alert to the wonder of being human. His students knew that, in spite of their flaws and shortcomings, they counted in his eyes for something important and worthwhile. He taught the bold and the shy and the bright and the slow, and he valued them all.

Jon was successful as a teacher in part because he remained, forever, a student himself. Reaching out beyond the borders of politics and government, he found excitement and wonder in art, in music, in literature and movies, in tennis, in languages, in every evidence of a full and creative life. He took courses in Latin and Greek, in Italian and Chinese; he played the

From right: Jon Reinhardt and David Evans receive awards for excellence in teaching at Convocation in 1970, the first of their kind ever given by the University.

violin; he drew and designed; he built furniture; he gave attention, both studious and carefree, to mind and body, to the senses and to the imagination. And, in all that he did, he was exuberantly alive, as if knowing that "exuberance is beauty."

But Jon was also successful as a teacher – and as a human being – because he understood that education is related to the moral conscience. He had the qualities of a gentleman – "a cultivated intellect, a delicate taste, … a courteous bearing" – but he also exalted virtue. And therefore he was immediately and permanently at home in this 150-year-old school which has endured in strength not alone because of learning but because of learning infused with virtue and faith.

I speak hesitantly of Jon as husband, as father, as son, as brother, for I would not trespass upon that deeply and intensely personal domain which is the life of a family. But I am sure, when I look at Dottie and Brett and Brooke and the Reinhardt family, that I see an environment of love, and I am sure that Jon's compassion, his vibrancy, and his gentleness of spirit will bring to all their remembrances of him a sweetness and a blessedness that will redeem future hours.

"The innocent and the beautiful," said Yeats, "have no enemy but Time." Time, is, we know, an adversary of unexampled power, and in the last six months we have seen the strength of time against someone we loved. But in quiet moments like these we hear other signals: vague and uncertain and fleeting, perhaps, but nonetheless appropriate to Jon Reinhardt and to what he lived for and believed in.

At the end of James Agee's novel *A Death in the Family*, the little boy Rufus, whose father has died, soon and suddenly, thinks of questions he would like to ask his uncle, but he is afraid to speak. Instead, he looks into his uncle's face, and does not ask, and his uncle does not speak, except to say, after a few minutes, "It's time to go home."

The Psalmist asks, "Who shall ascend into the hill of the Lord? Or who shall stand in his holy place? He that hath clean hands and a pure heart."

Today we remember with love a man of "clean hands, and a pure heart." A week ago he was in the hospital, desperately ill, but attentively grading the final examinations of his last courses.

On Monday, in an act of great affection and great courage, he was here, outdoors, on the campus to see the graduation of his son. On Thursday, just two days ago, somehow and mysteriously, the time came for him to "go home."

May 26, 1984

Harold W. Tribble

University President
Received the Medallion of Merit in 1984

THIS THIRTY-YEAR-OLD CHAPEL has been the setting for many Wake Forest convocations and ceremonies, but no event has fit more precisely the history and purpose of the place than these services for Harold Wayland Tribble. For it was he, more than any other person, who brought this chapel into being and who saw that it was located, majestically, here at the center of the campus. In honoring him today we also honor his achievement, and his achievement was nothing less than bringing to a grand fulfillment the concept and design of a university to be built here on this knoll in Forsyth County.

The vision of Wake Forest in Winston-Salem was not Harold Tribble's, to begin with. Others before him had signed agreements and made plans. But the vision became Dr. Tribble's own personal dream from the time he assumed the presidency in 1950. If the Trustees and the Convention and other Wake Foresters seriously wanted the new campus, they could have found no leader more willing, against all obstacles, to build it. In 1951, just outside this chapel, ground was broken; in 1953, cornerstones were laid; and in 1956 offices and classrooms and dormitories were occupied by students and faculty members marching westward. Wake Forest was suddenly – and rather surprisingly – here, and the old campus was on its way to becoming a distant memory.

There were eleven more years in Harold Tribble's presidency, and each of them brought new evidence of his strength, his courage, and his determination. He had his critics – he even had some enemies, I suppose – and, like others in authority, he doubtless made mistakes. But he was convinced that the path of his intentions was the right path for Wake Forest, and he let no one – faculty members, students, trustees, alumni, Baptist ministers, or corporation executives – swerve him from it. We know now that on the major issues confronting Wake Forest he was unflinchingly right. Evidence of his wisdom is everywhere to be seen, whether we explore the buildings of the campus or the minds and values of Wake Forest's alumni.

From the achievements of President Tribble's Winston-Salem years I select two as important and as representative. One is essentially of the intellect; the other is of the spirit. In 1961 the Graduate School was started. It had other sponsors, to be sure, but only Dr. Tribble had the commitment and the sheer obstinacy necessary for its establishment. His belief in the urgency of graduate programs for Wake Forest assured their beginnings and, in the long run, their survival.

On a second issue he was comparably firm: the right of every faculty and staff member to academic freedom. No less than his great predecessor, William Louis Poteat, though with a manner and style quite different, he saw Wake Forest as an instrument in the continuing search for truth, and for him that implied the privileges and powers of the individual conscience. Even when his

President Tribble with student

own tenaciously held religious convictions or the logic of community politics might have led him in a contrary direction, he ultimately emerged on the side of the liberated mind. He thereby affirmed and renewed Wake Forest's particular and unique destiny in Baptist educational history.

President Tribble declares to the Baptist State Convention that Wake Forest will not compromise its academic freedom.

Almost coincident with his retirement in 1967 Wake Forest became, in name, what it had already, in fact and in mission, become: a university. If Samuel Wait is to be remembered as the symbolic founder of Wake Forest College in Wake Forest, then surely we must remember Harold Tribble as the symbolic founder of Wake Forest University in Winston-Salem.

His mission finished, Harold Tribble retired. Like another Baptist president, Harry Truman, who left Washington for Independence and a quiet life with Bess, Dr. Tribble left Winston-Salem for his own "Independence" and a quiet life with Nelle, the loyal and beloved wife who had shared, unostentatiously, the burdens and the joys of his seventeen-year presidency. As far as I know, they were content in their departing and never looked back.

For me – and, I think, for others – a new insight into the character of Harold Tribble came with his retirement. We had known that he was an ambitious and aggressive man and that his purpose for Wake Forest was unyielding. Perhaps, we had thought in those moments when he stood proud and alone, he was, like most men, also seeking recognition and glory for himself. I have come to believe that earthly honors and rewards meant little to Dr. Tribble. He surely found pleasure, as anyone would, in the classroom building that bears his name, in the portrait that hangs in the Trustees' room, and in the pages of the Wake Forest story that are illuminated by his deeds. But he did not, I think, see the greatness of Wake Forest as in any way a testimonial to him. Rather, he saw Wake Forest as a testimonial to faith. And he knew that the rewards of faith, like the rewards of devoted service, are not in man's power to give. He was satisfied that the treasures he most fervently sought were elsewhere to be found.

June 19, 1986

K.A.N. Luther
Business Faculty

WHEN I THINK OF K.A.N. LUTHER, I think of the word "harmony." I hear it in the music which opened this service of celebration. I see it in my memory of his unforgettable countenance: intent, listening, and serene. I feel it, now, in the spirit which binds together all of us who knew and loved him. I sense it as I reflect upon the healing influence of his life.

K.A.N. understood the world better than most of us. He knew it, and he held it close. His reverence for India, the land of his ancestors; his love for Kenya, the place of his birth and childhood; his devotion to England, the country whose language and literature he embraced; his admiration for America, the nation of his career and his citizenship: his new-found appreciation for Japan and China, where he opened doors for his students and for his University: wherever K.A.N. Luther lived and traveled, he was at home. To him, there were no aliens. Beyond boundaries, he seemed to say to us, we are, in fact, one world and one people.

In his teaching and his scholarship also, K.A.N. sought unity. His fields of primary study were finance and economics, but he reached out beyond discipline in the same way he reached out beyond nationality and race. To his classes in management he brought the humane insights of liberal learning and culture, and to his assignments in the larger University he brought the practical, realistic judgment of a man who, for all his idealism, interpreted the working world as it really is.

The last time I saw K.A.N. Luther, he was in the hospital, and I knew – and he knew – that death was near. His wife Annette had been reading to him from the poetry of Emily Dickinson:

We never know how high we are
Till we are asked to rise
And then if we are true to plan
Our statures touch the skies –

As I looked at K.A.N. I knew that I was in the presence of a man who, in Emily Dickinson's word, had climbed "high." In youth he had ascended Kilimanjaro. In maturity he had made his way to the top of other mountains. Now, with the same adventurous spirit, with the same courage – "with an eye made quiet by the power of harmony, and the deep power of joy" – he was ready for the skies.

January 22, 1988

Harold Hayes

Alumnus, Board of Visitors
Received the Medallion of Merit in 1970

These remarks were given at a University ceremony in his memory.

1946 WAS A YEAR OF magic and exaltation. The war had ended, we celebrated victory, and we were home again. "Home" meant the house where our parents lived; for some of us it also meant Wake Forest, a quiet and green and sometimes radiant little college town. Wake Forest was, for the several years we went to school there, the "first place on earth."

Among the Wake Forest students of that magical year no one was more magical than Harold Hayes. Most of us were fairly plain and ordinary fellows; Harold was dashingly good-looking. Most of us were smart enough; Harold was so smart that he could afford to be casual about his smartness. Some of us had talent; Harold had talent too, but he also had style, nonchalance, grace. We wondered where it came from: this style. How could the son of a North Carolina Baptist minister have caught on, at such an early age, to the ways of a sophisticated world?

When the first issue of the 1948-49 *Student* appeared, under Harold's editorship, we knew at once that something provocative and revolutionary had happened to the College's old and respected literary magazine. From the cover illustration by Ralph Herring through Walt Friedenberg's article on the city jail and Bill McIlwain's "legend" about "The Man Who Ate Fried Cat" to Bill Hensley's and Leldon Kirk's record reviews and a pin-up photograph of Betty Isbell, we were looking at pictures and reading stories that we were not accustomed to finding in a Wake Forest publication. This new magazine had lightness and wit and spontaneity, but it also had an editorial control derived from exactingly professional literary and artistic standards. The editor was himself an accomplished writer: read again the piece he did on Dizzy Gillespie's bringing his court to Wake Forest. But he also knew other good writers when he saw them and he brought them to his staff. He understood how, in the same issue, to blend the serious, the ironic, and the comic, and he knew how to put together the entire magazine in such a way that it produced a unified impression about the Wake Forest College which was its central theme.

We thought that a new era for Wake Forest publications had begun, but in fact the era ended quickly, after the graduation of Harold Hayes and his fellow pranksters, and not again since the late 1940s has a literary magazine appeared at Wake Forest of such vitality and of such imaginative power. The concept – the energy, the "new look" – instead went with Harold Hayes to New York, where, on larger pages and to a world audience, it reappeared as the new *Esquire*, a magazine that under Harold's sensitive and creative editorship became for the America of the 1960s and 1970s what *The Student* had been for the Wake Forest of the 1940s.

During the years Harold worked in New York I saw him regularly – either in the big city, at alumni meetings or at development functions, or here in Winston-Salem, where he came for meetings of the College Board of Visitors, which he chaired, or for other University occasions. He introduced Wake Forest to New York friends – like Ralph Ellison and Martin Mayer – and they became our friends. He entertained us with stories about Manhattan and the literary scene and the urbane and talented people he knew. But what I most admired about Harold was that, inside, he never changed. If on the small town campus he had been a man of the world, in New York he was still a man of North Carolina: attentive to old friends and old associations, unpretentious, boyish, even provincial. The blend of artlessness and elegance, of sincerity and penetrating perceptiveness, manners which were both polished and natural – they were consistent in Harold from first to last. His life had unity. And it had something more. I don't know what "lonely impulse of delight" drove Harold to what he called the "last place on earth."

He said that, if he had not gone, he "might have lived out an otherwise self-absorbed life." What he discovered in Africa, he told us, was something "impenetrably mysterious" and "awesomely complex." I agree that the Serengeti and the animals who live there are "mysterious" and "complex" but no more so, I think, than the man who wrote those words about them. Harold, far from being "self-absorbed," was a man who, in his search for words, for truth, for friendship, for love, also transcended self. And whether he walked the paths of a once-upon-a-time North Carolina campus or the streets of a crowded New York or California city or the plains of a remote African plateau, he linked his own identity with his human and his natural surroundings. In those surroundings, I think, he found and fulfilled himself, and through his search and his discovery he also helped us to understand ourselves.

More than most of us, he saw

That Light whose smile kindles the Universe,
That Beauty in which all things work and move
… that sustaining Love
Which through the web of being blindly wove
By man and beast and earth and air and sea,
Burns bright or dim, as each are mirrors of
The fire for which all thirst…*

April 18, 1989

*These lines of poetry are from Percy Bysshe Shelley.

Carlton Prince West
History Faculty, Librarian

To the little college town of Wake Forest, North Carolina, where almost everyone, teacher and student, was Southern-born and Southern-bred and where unmistakably Southern accents and cadences supplied the sounds and the rhythms of conversation, Carlton West brought a different voice: the voice of his native

New England, where he had lived until that milestone day in 1928 when he had come to Wake Forest to teach history. With that voice – clear, precise, never fuzzy or unfocused, always pure in tone and emphasis – he lectured to generations of Wake Forest undergraduates. So remarkable, in fact, were his gifts as a teacher that even students who were not enrolled in his sections gathered once a week in a large lecture room to hear him speak. I know, because I was one of those students. And more than fifty years later I vividly recall seeing him – and hearing him – from my assigned chair in the big room of the Social Science Building. He spoke with conviction and assurance, and for those of us who had never left our Southern homes, there was, in how he spoke and what he said, something of the distant authority we had come to associate with Emerson and Hawthorne and the golden years of New England learning. Mr. West was a welcome visitor in our midst.

The skills – as teacher, as speaker – that Carlton West brought to Wake

Forest as that "visitor" never left him during the sixty-three years he lived among us – no longer a "visitor" but an adopted son who came to love the South and to love Wake Forest and who chose to spend his life here, even in retirement. Just a year ago this month, in what, I think, was his last public appearance, he spoke – without notes, but in polished phrases, and with fact and feeling – about his library colleague, Margaret Wallace, who was then beginning her own retirement. The voice, the gestures, the manner were the same as ever: still strong, still dignified.

The wisdom and the academic sophistication that characterized everything Mr. West did for Wake Forest inspired him in the late 1930s to undertake a study of the College, preparatory to an application for a chapter of Phi Beta Kappa. Mr. West later remembered that the study took him six months to complete and required more than two hundred pages of text. He was successful, and on January 13, 1941, in the Philomathesian Literary Society room in Wait Hall, the Wake

Forest chapter of Phi Beta Kappa – Delta of North Carolina – was installed. Mr. West's labors had, to use Wake Forest historian George Paschal's word, "secured" this chapter, and it is a measure of Mr. West's achievement that no North Carolina college has been added to Phi Beta Kappa's roster during the intervening half-century.

Most of you here at these services this afternoon perhaps knew Mr. West best from his years as librarian. He accepted this position in the same year, 1946, in which the move to Winston-Salem was announced; oversaw the expedition that brought books, periodicals, and people to our new home in Forsyth County; and until his retirement in 1975 worked with diligence and modesty to develop a great library for reading and research. Mr. West knew books, he read books, he loved books, he liked being surrounded by books; and so he was at home in the library. But his labors there were undertaken without self-importance, and his achievements were arrived at without fanfare. As he was respectful toward books, so was he respectful toward people: courteous and kind. Some of you here today, I am sure, could cite evidences of his calm and unostentatious concern for his staff and his friends.

Mr. West once said of himself, "I am the type of person who can work and be happy alone.... I'm not the kind of person who hangs around watching what's done and commenting." He was often, by his own choice, alone. But friends who knew him well remember that in moments of relaxation he was witty and urbane. He sang, he played the piano, he painted, he did genealogical research, he wrote, he appreciated and protected trees, he was a lively dinner companion. On the old campus there was a table in one of the local boarding houses where, every night during the week, eight or ten friends would gather for the evening meal and for conversation. I was never privileged to be a member of this circle, but I have heard about the discussions these men and women had and about Mr. West's contributions: high-minded, perceptive, serious or more likely amusing, always sane.

Carlton West's roots were on that "stern and rock-bound coast" to which in 1620 the Mayflower Pilgrims came, and, fittingly, his ashes will return there – to the state of his ancestors and the land of his own birth and boyhood. But let us claim, for North Carolina and for Wake Forest, a portion of his genial and faithful spirit, and let us remember him as one who, for the larger part of a century, lived in this good place and called it home.

June 20, 1991

Allen Easley

Alumnus, Religion Faculty
Received the Medallion of Merit in 1972

ANY PERSON IS BLESSED who, even once in a lifetime, meets – and then has as a friend – someone who represents what a human being truly ought to be. For me – and for many of you and for others, past and present, not here today – Allen Easley was such a human being, and we can be profoundly grateful that he lived 64 of his 99 years at Wake Forest, a familiar and graciously accessible symbol of the possibilities of life. This afternoon, in my mind's eye, I see him again as I have so often seen him: his face strong and handsome; his eyes clear and focused; listening to what is being said, and listening appreciatively; eager to endow us all with the gift of his attention. Do you remember the look he had in conversation? (Of course you do.) He was so concerned with what you had to say: his eyes would sparkle, he would make some gesture of approval with his hand or his head, and you would feel somehow accepted and important – as if you counted for more than you knew. He gave to us out of his own dignity, and our dignity became thereby enlarged. I have never known a man with a better face.

The source of this so well remembered charm was, I think, in the rare ability he had to create around himself a circle of warmth and comfort within which others could at once feel relaxed and at home. He had the talent of suggesting that in his presence everyone would be greeted with kindness and keen concentration. I used to marvel

From right: Allen Easley with President Scales

at the variety and extent of his friendships. A minister, a teacher of religion, he was unmistakably a man of deep religious convictions: we could not fail to notice that he was touched by an amazing grace that made him dutiful and serene. Fellow believers thus found their own faith confirmed in the fabric of his life; in him was made manifest the promise embodied in those grand phrases "the means of grace" and "the hope of glory."

And yet he was no less an available friend to those who did not believe as he did. Without arrogance or rebuke, he listened to them and offered them patience and understanding. How many sceptics must have found in him one man of holy offices whom they could approach without timidity or fear of criticism! I recall that, when Wake Forest moved to Winston-Salem, he was one of the first faculty members to become a true citizen of this new community. Some of you here this afternoon, I suspect, came to know and appreciate Wake Forest through Allen Easley, and your opinion of this strange college coming into your midst must have been lifted by your awareness that Allen Easley belonged to it and loved it.

It was, paradoxically, during the years of his so-called "retirement" that Allen Easley flourished most surprisingly. Beyond "three score and ten" he lived as if life were just beginning and horizons were unlimited. Especially did he find joy in art. Still a scholar in religion and sometimes still a preacher, he surrounded himself with paintings and drawings and art books, and he could speak with passion of a work by Rembrandt or Van Gogh or Cezanne that he had studied and found pleasure in. But for him the living present was also a source of aesthetic appeal, and he made it abundantly clear that his appreciation for the new, the artistically innovative was genuine and eager. His own impulses toward creativity led him in his seventies to become a studio art student himself, and most of us are familiar with the works that resulted: their precision, their inventiveness, their delicate balance between tradition and experiment.

His love of art was only one facet of his intense awareness of the beauty of the world around him. He found inspiration also in literature – in Shakespeare, in Emily Dickinson, in Browning (whom he had read intently since college days) – and in music and flowers, so much a part of the happy life he and Madge lived together for forty-one years. This afternoon, as we pay tribute to Allen, we also continue to praise Madge, still very much in our recollections: her graciousness, her own devotion to beauty, her fierce loyalties, her lack of pretentiousness, her steadfast love for Allen. And we praise that other remarkable woman Nell Robertson Easley, the mother of the four Easley children – children, I am happy to say, of my own Wake Forest generation.

Allen and Madge Easley

Each of you has his (or her) favorite remembrances of Allen Easley, and many of your memories, like mine, have as their setting a classroom, a faculty meeting, a festive dining room, a living room with a fire blazing brightly, a back yard or garden on a summer day. Today I see him, for example, standing here in this place to pray or to read Scripture: sitting in a faculty Executive Committee meeting (next to Forrest Clonts or Lewis Aycock or Jasper Memory or another long-time colleague); undertaking with good will the supervision of another Southern Association Self-Study – a tedious task at best; rising with power in a College faculty meeting to say with victorious conviction that the days of racial segregation at Wake Forest must come to an end; celebrating another milestone birthday (his 80th or his 85th or his 90th or his 95th) with impeccably clear memory and with impeccably courteous manners.

I also recall four trips that he and Mark Reece and sometimes Anne Mercer Shields and I – and several other colleagues and students – took to New York to buy works of art for the Student Union collection. The first of these took place in 1963, the year of his retirement; the fourth one occurred when he was 84. As a non-voting lay member I mostly watched and listened as Dr. Easley and the others, moving from gallery to gallery, debated the quality and price of the paintings and prints on display. After a crowded day of walking and looking we would go to a play or an opera and then return to our hotel for further discussion. It would be inaccurate to say that Dr. Easley kept pace with the rest of us during those grueling days: he set the pace which we had to struggle to maintain. At the end of one long and successful day, I remember, we were separating for a night's rest, Dr. Easley was leaving the room, and a young woman student turned to me and said, "I love that man." She spoke for all of us on that committee – and, of course, for all of us here this afternoon.

Charlotte said to me the other day – the day on which her father died – "he was a dear." He was "a dear" – especially to Jack and Charlotte and Nancy and Eleanor and their children and grandchildren – but also to each one of us whom he called friend. And, as we ponder his life and his character, we must not forget, even on an occasion as serious as this one, that he was a happy, a light-hearted and merry man whom we should pay homage to with a smile.

Allen Easley liked, and now and then quoted, the poems of A.A. Milne, and these poems have haunted my imagination ever since I heard that Allen had died.

Let it rain! Who cares? I've a train upstairs!
Where am I going? The high rooks call:
"It's awful fun to be born at all." Where am I going? The ring-doves coo:
"We do have beautiful things to do."

And, best of all, one of Allen's favorite poems:

They're changing guard at Buckingham Palace
– Christopher Robin went down with Alice.
"Do you think the King knows all about me?"
"Sure to, dear, but it's time for tea."

On this summer afternoon, as tea time approaches, I think of Allen Easley, your friend and mine, coming to the King's "Palace" just in time for the changing of the guard and being welcomed into the Palace by the King. And the King says, "I know all about you, Allen Easley. We have beautiful things to do. Come in."

July 6, 1992

Don Schoonmaker

Alumnus, Political Science Faculty

THERE IS A PASSAGE in Thoreau's *Walden* that comes to my mind when I think of Don Schoonmaker. "To be awake," said Thoreau, "is to be alive. I have never yet met a man who was quite awake." Don Schoonmaker, as much as any person I have ever known, was "quite awake" and "alive." And this afternoon, as I remember him, I see him as still "awake" and "alive."

The first time I met Don, in 1957 in the Wake Forest cafeteria, I saw that he was "awake" to everything around him. Mainly I saw his smile: a little shy, a little amused, enormously appealing, inviting immediate confidence and friendship. I saw that same smile the last time I saw Don, just before he left for his final stay in the hospital. He had suffered, more than I knew, but the smile was there: no less warm, no less "awake" to life. And I think I saw, around the edges of the smile, the same amusement: a gentle mixture of joy and irony.

For Don was a happy man. And he

was happy, I think, because he had courage: so much courage that his heart was never divided. Long before most white men recognized that there was even a problem, Don Schoonmaker stood – publicly and passionately – for liberty and justice for all. To say that he was "without prejudice" would be to belittle his commitments. His strength in civil and human rights was a positive strength: founded on a love for humanity that transcended color and gender and social status and that embraced all life and all those who live life. His home and his heart were always open to whoever came: from next door, from across town, from North or South, or from some distant land. There were no barriers to Don's affection. Don showed the same courage as a faculty member at Wake Forest. An institution, if it is to be strong and true, needs loyal critics as much as it needs faithful defenders. But most critics of an institution speak only in safe houses among trusted friends.

Don spoke where he could be most clearly heard by those who he thought most needed to hear: in faculty meetings, from his seat on the aisle on the right-hand side of DeTamble Auditorium. He inquired, he probed, he challenged – but never in anger or in malice and never from any hope for personal gain. He spoke because he wanted the University he loved and served to be virtuous. And he always ended his questions with a smile.

In so many ways, of course, Don was, unabashedly and whole-heartedly, a "liberal." And yet, in so many other ways, he was deeply conservative, especially among those he dearly loved. He was infinitely loyal: to his wife, Meyressa, the college sweetheart whom he fell in love with a long time ago and whom he, forever after, loved with impeccable devotion; to his children, Kirsten and Trevor, who already, in the maturity of their early twenties, show the same courage and compassion that Don and Meyressa have had; and to the many students whom he taught, counseled, and loved. The symbolic memory remains with me of the home movie Don made with and for the students who were with him in Venice: the easy and natural community between him and his students was evidence of lasting bonds built on respect and good humor. Don talked and listened and inspired and cared, and the students quickly became members of Don's family: a family from which no one

Schoonmaker (2nd from right) with colleagues in 1980.

was excluded and in which there was always room for another.

Don was also infinitely loyal to his friends, young and old. Many of us here today, I believe, can say that we have never had a more trusted – or more faithful – friend than Don. Certainly, I can say that. But Don's friendship was never a burden, as even close friendships can sometimes be. His friendship was always a blessing: it grew out of an unfailing zest for life, and it asked nothing in return. To be with Don was to experience the sweetness of the familiar and the joy of the newly discovered. Another birthday showing of Charlie Chaplin's Modern Times (I had looked forward to that celebration again this year), the recollection of often quoted lines from De Tocqueville, a barbecue sandwich at Simos' (with a slice of tomato brought from his own garden) – these already ordinary things – were somehow still fresh and miraculous and to be savored once again. A new movie just opened at the Janus in Greensboro, a paperback book (never read before) by an Italo Calvino or an Octavio Paz, the way in which a touch of basil can bring new life to food: these were revelations that gave life vitality and excitement and were always to be shared and talked about and pondered over.

For not only was Don "awake" and "alive"; he made others "awake" and "alive." Don often read the poems and letters of John Keats, a writer who, like Don, knew illness and suffering, who died long before he should have died, but who found joy in the process of life itself as long as life lasted: in "the rainbow of the salt sand-wave", in "Fast fading violets cover'd up in leaves"; in "The reading of an ever-changing tale; / The light uplifting of a maiden's veil; / A pigeon tumbling in clear summer air; / A laughing school-boy, without grief or care, / Riding the springy branches of an elm."

"A laughing school-boy, without grief or care": that is how I finally remember my friend Don Schoonmaker this afternoon. To be sure, he grew up, and he experienced "grief" and "care." But he overcame grief and care, and the image of laughter – the school-boy, the grown man, the husband, the father, the friend remains. Don is, for me, still awake, still alive – just as Keats was for Shelley when Shelley wrote:

Peace, peace! he is not dead, he doth not sleep,
   He hath awakened from the dream of life,
He is a portion of the loveliness
   Which once he made more lovely:
He is a presence to be felt and known
   In darkness and in light,

May 23, 1993

Lois Johnson

Dean of Women
Received the Medallion of Merit in 1973

LOIS JOHNSON HAS A PLACE IN Wake Forest history that is honored and unique.

Yesterday morning, just as I was leaving my office for a reunion meeting of Wake Forest's Class of 1943, I heard the news of Miss Lois Johnson's death. At any time those tidings would have been sad and would have immediately brought forth many memories of Wake Forest, old and new, but on this anniversary occasion they were especially poignant. For the Class of 1943 – my class – was the first Wake Forest class to be coeducational, and it was at the beginning of our senior year that Miss Johnson was named Wake Forest's first Dean of Women. She became – at once – our friend, our counselor, and the embodiment of Wake Forest ideals.

Our reunion programs continued late last night, and I regret not having had time to begin to do justice to Miss Johnson's years at Wake Forest or to the influence she had on so many of us. She deserves a tribute extended and eloquent and loving. I fear that mine will be far too inadequate.

Miss Johnson – for me and for many – had every good quality that counts in a human being. She was lovely and charming and dignified: the authentic representation of an authentic Southern woman. In her presence, whether we were students or colleagues, we knew that manners were important and that codes of conduct were to be respected. She had the magical ability of conveying, simultaneously, authority and kindness, and she created around herself an atmosphere that invited both admiration and relaxation.

Miss Johnson liked to read, and her alert mind responded to all evidences of subtlety and wit in a book. She was often amused by fiction – and by life – and her smile confirmed a playfulness of spirit that surprised and delighted those who might have first encountered her as a figure of command.

You of the Wagram-Riverton community know far better than I of Miss Johnson's devotion to her large and talented extended family and her life-long nurturing as a Southern Baptist in the honorable liberal traditions of that vibrant denomination. I recall also because we talked about politics many times and, I might add, were always in agreement – her loyalty, through good times and bad, to the Democratic party.

At Wake Forest, first on the old campus and then on the new, there is a dormitory named in Miss Johnson's honor. Her portrait – an especially good one which captures both her beauty and her sense of humor – is hung prominently so that alumni can see her when they visit the campus. Our archives are filled with her name and her picture. I remember especially a photograph of her and Jasper Memory on the cover of an alumni magazine: they were receiving the University's highest honor, the Medallion of Merit.

Lois Johnson and Jasper Memory receive the Medallion of Merit.

But it is in our hearts that the face, the life, the style of Lois Johnson will be most faithfully reproduced. The poet Wordsworth once wrote of the woman he loved and married: she was

A perfect Woman, nobly planned,
To warm, to comfort, and command;
And yet a spirit still, and bright
With something of angelic light.

Dean Johnson reminiscing at a reunion with Beth Perry Upchurch, the first regularly enrolled coed (left), and Martha Ann Allen Turnage, first female editor of the Old Gold and Black.

Today on the Wake Forest campus we are celebrating Homecoming for thousands of alumni who have returned to places and people they knew and loved. Here, in Wagram, we celebrate another Homecoming: the coming home of a gallant woman who continues to illuminate our memories and our lives with "something of angelic light."

October 23, 1993

Iona Wells Speas

Reference Librarian, Wife of Professor William Speas

THE "TIE THAT BINDS" ALL OF us who knew Wake Forest College forty or fifty years ago is strong and "blest." And whenever anyone from our "happy band" of brothers and sisters dies, we are not only saddened but also somehow diminished in ourselves. Another link to our past is broken; one less person is with us who remembers what we knew and loved.

Iona Speas was a young wife and mother in that academic village of our past. In her home on Woodland Drive, in what was then the "new" part of town, a place filled with trees, still a little wild, not so far away from the College and yet somehow remote, she and her professor husband and their three gifted daughters were made aware every day of the natural beauty of plants and flowers and also of the inexhaustible pleasures to be found in books and in music.

Dr. "Bill" Speas taught physics, and no one who studied under Dr. Speas ever forgot him. His lectures were provocative, his classroom and laboratory experiments lively, his wit unmatched. Stories about him were told anew to every freshman class – stories that were always funny and always admiring. With little money and limited equipment, and often by himself, Dr. Speas laid the foundation of physics at Wake Forest, and he laid it with wisdom and a smile.

Iona Speas was a faculty wife: renting rooms to students, working with the University Club from its beginnings, singing in the church choir, available for whatever college duties came her way. (In old Wake Forest, everybody counted, and everybody was needed and appreciated.) But she also had a professional life of her own: teaching in elementary school and, later, working as a reference librarian at the College. Once, I have been told, when she was still Iona Wells, she took her fourth grade students to the College observatory to hear a lecture on the stars by Professor Speas. The students, reportedly, saw many stars that night; Dr. Speas, however, said he saw only one star: Iona.

Bill and Iona Speas, together with most of their best Wake Forest friends, came to Winston-Salem in 1956 and recreated, in the classrooms and laboratories of Salem Hall and in their new home on Faculty Drive, the life they had known on the old campus. Dr. Speas lived for only five more years, but Iona continued in resilience and good cheer until that moment last Monday when she went quietly to sleep.

Such was the life of Iona Speas, but it does not begin to define or explain her. We must look elsewhere for guidance. I turn to two passages from Scripture. First: "Consider the lilies of the field, how they grow; they toil not, neither do they spin: And yet I say unto you, that even Solomon in all his glory was not arrayed like one of these." And second: "Suffer little children, and forbid them not, to come unto me: for of such is the kingdom of heaven."

Iona Speas did indeed "consider the lilies of the field," and she also "considered" (and sometimes borrowed) the magnolias of the campus, as well as every other flower that bloomed and blossomed. Someone once said of her that, if a great flood came and washed away everything but one flower, she would see not the devastation but the flower. It was beauty that she looked for in life, and it was beauty that she found.

And she also "suffered" little children to come unto her. With a smile that warmed, a laugh that made happy, and stories that captured attention, she was at home with children. Perhaps she understood children because in some charming way she remained a child herself – not from a lack of wisdom and maturity, for she was a wise and mature woman, but in gentleness and in hope and in faith. The sparkle of youth in her never disappeared.

Just two months ago, Alice and Melinda and Frances came to celebrate their mother's ninetieth birthday – with piano and voice and flute. I like to think now of Iona Speas on that day: appreciating the flowers and friends around her, listening to music that she loved, and seeing before her those three gifted daughters, now grown and now mothers themselves, whom she and Dr. Bill once upon a time brought into abundant life and to whom they gave a legacy richer than Solomon's.

August 27, 1994

L. H. Hollingsworth
Alumnus, Chaplain

EVERY NOW AND THEN someone appears in the life of an institution who, because of certain distinctive and unique personal qualities, becomes a conspicuous and visible campus figure about whom stories are told, memories are shared, and legends are developed. Leon H. Hollingsworth – or "Holly," as I shall call him today, even in this formal setting – was such a person.

In the last few days I have of course been thinking much about Holly, and I have been trying somehow to put into words what there was about him that made him loom so large in the modern life of Wake Forest. And remembering him, I have found myself, not surprisingly, being drawn to the familiar opening lines of the Wake Forest "Alma Mater:" "Dear old Wake Forest! Thine is a noble name; Thine is a glorious fame, Constant and true."

Holly loved Wake Forest without reservation, and for more than fifty years he was, in the words of our fight song, a "herald" of her story. Even as an undergraduate – a classmate of mine on the old campus, I am grateful to say – he understood and absorbed what Wake Forest meant.

He knew that a way of life had been developed and nurtured at Wake Forest that was a magical blend of intellect and faith, of the mind and the spirit, and that permeated the entire campus: from classrooms to church and chapel to dormitory and gymnasium. He had a maturity of insight both about Wake Forest and about his own vocation that derived partly from his being somewhat older and more experienced than most of us; from his already being married to his lovely Bess, a welcome classmate of ours on a still mostly male campus; but also from an inner yearning for harmony and reconciliation among people of different assumptions and ambitions.

During his years away from Wake Forest, in the Army and in church pastorates, he never forgot Wake Forest, and he spoke for us, honestly and courageously, in those places across North Carolina where Baptists gathered. He was always our friend – a friend who knew our faults, as parents know the faults of sons and daughters, but none the less our advocate. And it was as our advocate and friend that he came home in 1959 to be our chaplain.

Ed Christman has spoken, from a perspective I cannot claim, about Holly's eleven years as chaplain. I will say only that, on the many Tuesdays and Thursdays I was in attendance in chapel, I was impressed by the way in which Holly filled the pulpit – both his person and his voice conveyed largeness and power – and by the way in which he sought a rich and often exhilarating variety in programming and presentation. He was always generous to guests, whoever they were.

Officially, Holly left Wake Forest in 1970. But – and I consider this perhaps the greatest evidence of his undying love for Wake Forest – he never really left. Wherever he went, whatever other positions and responsibilities he had, Wake Forest remained "home," and whenever Wake Forest called, he answered. We heard his strong and clear voice as he spoke his beautifully crafted prayers, each one of them a jewel in composition. We saw him at banquets, at Homecoming events, wherever Wake Forest Deacons assembled, and we watched him move around, recognizing a face, remembering a story, offering laughter or sympathy as needed. And we felt, in all these encounters, his innate kindness and his unburdened love of life.

This past Saturday night, at the annual Sports Hall of Fame induction banquet, Holly's spirit was much in evidence. It may well have been the first such occasion he had ever missed. But from the speaker's table, he was honored, and, wherever alumni shook hands and talked, he was remembered. For we knew, whether we came from academics or athletics, that Holly cherished us all and that nothing would have pleased him more than to have seen us, as friends and alumni, uniting to praise Wake Forest men and women.

Chaplain Hollingsworth with students

After all, that had been one of his most steadfast purposes in life: to say, with a conviction that never faltered, "Dear old Wake Forest! Thine is a noble name; Thine is a glorious fame, Constant and true!" "Constant and true": what better words could we find to describe and honor this dear friend whose life we celebrate this morning?

February 27, 1995

Lucile Aycock

Information Desk, Wife of Professor Lewis Aycock

A LITTLE MORE THAN SEVENTEEN YEARS AGO, many of us gathered in Wait Chapel to remember and to praise one of the truest and most honorable servants Wake Forest has known: Andrew Lewis Aycock, Professor of English, visionary founder of our program in art history, a man of gentle strength and a kind heart who represented – on both campuses, old and new – what was best and most lasting about Wake Forest.

I had the honor of speaking on that occasion, and I recall saying that Professor Aycock was a man who was at peace with himself but that much of the obvious happiness that radiated from him came from his "beloved wife Lucile." Today we – family and friends – gather again, this time to remember and praise Lucile Aycock. The seventeen years that have passed have taken from us many Wake Forest men and women whom we loved and cherished, and there are fewer of us now who recall the bright years of the Aycocks. But they were bright years indeed, and Lucile Aycock had a radiance that complemented her husband's but that was also fully reflective of who she was.

In some ways, I suppose, they were different. He was more formal, more reserved; she more vivacious, more casual. He had the temperament of a

From right: Lucile Aycock and Mildred Brown on a Wake Forest outing

scholar; she liked the familiar routines of life. He often sought the quietness of office or library; she liked being in the middle of things.

Each of them had a distinctive personality.

But in the important ways, they were alike: in their absolute devotion to family (to daughters Delia and Jane, to sons-in-law, to grandchildren, to great-grandchildren); in their good cheer; in their kindness to others; in their deep-rooted integrity; in their transcendent faith.

I realize that so far I may seem to have spoken as much about Mr. Aycock as about Mrs. Aycock, but to me they were wonderfully inseparable, and I think – having known Mrs.

Aycock well and having lived in her home for one happy summer – that she would want her life within the family to be central to our memories of her.

But Mrs. Aycock had motivations and purposes in life that were uniquely her own. From her arrival in old Wake Forest in 1930 she was known and appreciated for her gifts of hospitality: for entertaining visitors with food and laughter and, if they were in need of temporary housing, even with a place to stay. Her daughters remember that their house was often full of people: students, with perhaps their parents; sons of missionaries, now far away from home; new faculty members being welcomed to the campus with characteristic Aycock courtesy; during the War, soldiers and their families. Sometimes Mrs. Aycock had to make the "loaves and fishes" that were available in the kitchen go a long way.

Mrs. Aycock's "unofficial" career as a generous hostess emerged in full flower on this campus – in Reynolda Hall, at the Information Desk, where, often with her dear friend Lib Griffin, she greeted students, teachers, visitors, whoever came by, with questions, answers, information, suggestions. Her sincerity, her enthusiasm, her unfailing desire to be of assistance: these were instantly communicated to both friends and newcomers, and many a person left her presence assured of having encountered in Mrs. Aycock someone who really cared. I think that no one at Wake Forest, during her years of service, saw and helped more people than she did. Even after her retirement she returned to work on special occasions like Homecoming, when the University wanted to be sure that returning alumni would receive the heartiest welcome possible. We were confident that Mrs. Aycock would know many of those who returned and would quickly find out who the strangers were.

Lucile Aycock genuinely loved life, and she was intensely loyal to the people and the institutions she believed in. In my memory today Mrs. Aycock remains smiling and alert. "Strength and honor" were, as the selection from the Book of Proverbs read by Bill Angell says, "her clothing." She looked "well to the ways of her household." "Her children arise up, and call her blessed." Let us therefore "Give her of the fruit of her hands; and let her own works praise her in the gates" that have now opened to receive her.

June 17, 1995

From left: Lucile Aycock with her information desk colleagues, William Holoman and Lib Griffin

Pendleton Banks

Anthropology Faculty

I BEGIN WITH SOME VERSES translated from the Sanskrit:

Listen to the Exhortation of the Dawn!
Look to this Day! for it is Life,
The very Life of Life.
In its brief course lie all the Verities
And all the Realities of your Existence;
The Bliss of Growth,
The Glory of Action,
The Splendor of Beauty;
For Yesterday is but a Dream
And Tomorrow is only a Vision;
But Today well lived
Makes every Yesterday a Dream of Happiness,
And every Tomorrow a Vision of Hope.
Look well, therefore, to this Day!
Such is the Salutation of the Dawn.

These lines were especially admired by Pen Banks. All of us who knew Pen can understand why. For he was an explorer, an adventurer who lived, each day as it came, with expectation and ever renewable vigor.

He must have been like that from the beginning. His children showed me several pieces he wrote for his college magazine when he was a senior. One of them, a short story, tells of a trip by steamer from Singapore to Kalong. Another – a poem – salutes the "fair bright [French] voice" of Francois Villon and asks the question: "Where is [now] the bold Charlemagne?"

I do not know whether it was Pen's

boyhood dreams of exploration or the voices he heard out of the distant past – or his years in the Navy, when, as he movingly recounted last year, he captained an LCT during the June 6, 1944 invasion of Europe – which destined him to study anthropology at Harvard and to bring the study of anthropology to Wake Forest.

Whatever the background causes may have been, however, we of Wake Forest are fortunate that in his thirty-first year Pen joined our own campus community. The impact of his presence for the next forty years was historic: he founded the Department of Anthropology, he started the Museum of Anthropology and – at a college still regional in outlook and perspective – he urged us to look abroad. Be bold, he said.

I know from many conversations with Pen how persuasive – and how tenacious – he could be. Administrators – and faculty members too – are sometimes slow to move, and Pen had to push hard to get what he wanted for the Department and for the Museum. But he never gave up, and his quiet persistence – he was steadfast but always polite and gentlemanly – produced the results he wanted. The strength of anthropology among our departments today and the reputation of our Museum are testimony to the vision and the labors of Pen Banks, as well as of those who followed him here.

But, as I have said, Pen's ambitions for Wake Forest were not confined to one department. He was an early and enthusiastic supporter of our Asian Studies program, and every time a new venture in International Studies was proposed, he was on hand to give encouragement and to participate. And – most exciting of all – he went himself: not just to safe and convenient places like Venice and the cultural centers of the West, but to Romania, to Yugoslavia, to China, to Burma, to Mongolia – wherever his dreams beckoned. Many of us, I suppose, wonder what it would be like to go where few Americans have gone and to see what few Americans have seen. Most of us don't go; perhaps we lack what Pen had in abundance: the courage, the

A Burmese monkey god reminds Professor Banks of his year in Rangoon as a Fulbright lecturer.

40 | *Songs of Wake Forest*

determination, to hear the "salutation of the dawn" and to answer its call.

A little more than a year ago Pen went back to England and to the continent of Europe to live again the dangers and the achievements of D-Day. This time he was accompanied by a large family: his wife Catherine, beloved companion of many years and many trips, and children and grandchildren – twenty Bankses in all. I consider that journey symbolic of Pen's life: still traveling, still forward-looking, yet surrounded by his devoted wife and family. Pen knew where adventure lay, but he also knew where home is, and after many wanderings he always came back to where he started from.

Alfred Tennyson imagined another explorer, Ulysses, nearing the end of his life, remembering his travels, but, as always, looking ahead:

Professor "Pen" Banks on one of his fairly frequent overseas trips, this time to Venezuela.

For always roaming with a hungry heart
Much have I seen and known; cities of men
And manners, climates, councils, governments,
Myself not least, but honour'd of them all;
. . . .

The lights begin to twinkle from the rocks:
The long day wanes: the slow moon climbs: the deep
Moans round with many voices. Come, my friends,
'Tis not too late to seek a newer world.
 Push off, and sitting well in order smite
The sounding furrows; for my purpose holds
To sail beyond the sunset, and the baths
Of all the western stars, until I die.
It may be that the gulfs will wash us down:
It may be we shall touch the Happy Isles,
And see the great Achilles, whom we knew.
Tho' much is taken, much abides; and tho'
We are not now that strength which in old days
Moved earth and heaven; that which we are, we are;
One equal temper of heroic hearts,
Made weak by time and fate, but strong in will
To strive, to seek, to find, and not to yield.
. . . .

August 18, 1995

James Ralph Scales

University President
Received the Medallion of Merit in 1984

WAKE FOREST MEN AND WOMEN, for all the years to come, will honor the name of James Ralph Scales. Like Wait and Wingate, like Taylor and Poteat, like Kitchin and Tribble, he too has now arrived at a final and secure place in Wake Forest history – not alone because for sixteen years he sat at the President's desk and did the President's business, but because he brought to the Presidency an exuberance and a spirit of adventure and – I think the word is right – a glamour the office had not known before.

The Scales personality was evident from the beginning. I remember the night in the Magnolia Room when he delivered his first major address here: a heartfelt tribute to his native state of Oklahoma, so eloquent and so loving that we in the audience could almost hear in the distance the Oklahoma wind come sweeping down the plain. President Scales always delighted in words, and he could use words unexpectedly: a turn here, a twist there, a glimmer, a teasing insight, words curiously crafted and often enigmatic. One could not always be sure exactly what he meant, but one knew that an original mind was at work with the instruments of language. There was content, of course, but there was also style, and there was playfulness. Dr. Scales liked to speak and to write – and he also liked just to talk.

He was, in fact, something of an actor. He enjoyed being "on stage" – in the center of things. So it is appropriate that the campus building which bears his name be the Fine Arts Center. Look closely at that building, with its public spaces inside and outside, its lobbies and studios, its theatres and recital hall, and notice all around you features and graces that delight the eye. That building may well be Dr. Scales's most important material gift to Wake Forest: he made it the first priority of his presidency and, with the faithful and brilliant guidance of Charles Allen, saw it to completion. Look again at Anne Shields' inviting full-length portrait of Dr. Scales – startlingly alive, friendly but commanding – which presides over the lobby of the music building. He is at home in that place, and there he will be looked up to by students and visitors of the future who never had the pleasure that we have had of knowing him in the flesh.

Fourth building from right: Casa Artom, Wake Forest's first overseas house

Dr. Scales had cosmopolitan tastes – he liked to travel and he liked settings of comfort and sophistication – and so, acting almost entirely on his own, he decided that Wake Forest should have colonies: overseas programs, first in Venice and next in London. The spirit of James Ralph Scales haunts both these cities, and those of you who have looked out onto the Grand Canal from the upstairs living room of Casa Artom or left Worrell House to walk down Steeles Road toward the Chalk Farm Underground should remember that Dr. Scales is the sponsor of your pleasures. I traveled with him both to Venice and to London, and I know what a good companion he was: alert, attentive to every sight, savoring the pleasure of tea rooms and restaurants and clubs: a connoisseur of "the good life."

But the main business of Dr. Scales's administration was back home in Winston-Salem, and under his leadership Wake Forest became stronger and better and more free. There were occasional crises, especially during the unsettling and sometimes turbulent years of the late sixties and early seventies, but Dr. Scales, an experienced naval officer from years on an aircraft carrier in World War II, was a calm and shrewd navigator, and the University reached port not only without damage but with renewed seaworthiness. Facts and statistics and administrative decisions could be cited to define further the Scales years, but Scales the president is to be found in the records, and today I would speak primarily of Scales the man and Scales my friend.

One of the characters in a James M. Barrie play, when asked the question "What is charm?", replied, "If you have it, you don't need to have anything else; and if you don't have it, it doesn't much matter what else you have." Well, Dr. Scales had other qualities – intelligence and wit a-plenty – but he also had "charm," and that is what many of us will remember most of all. He could walk across the campus, move in and out of offices, visit the cafeteria or the library, see a play or hear a concert, and everywhere he went, he stopped to talk, to ask how people were. Class and race and conditions of employment were never barriers to his friendship or his compassionate concern. He genuinely liked being with people, and people genuinely liked being with him. Also, he never wanted to offend. How often, when he feared he had said or done something improper, have I heard him say "So sorry."

How did this president of admittedly patrician inclinations remain so thoroughly a man of the people? In part, I think, because he continued to be an old-fashioned liberal. Brought up in the inspirational and hopeful years of Franklin Roosevelt's New Deal, tempered by the progressive patriotic virtues proclaimed in World War II, he believed passionately in democracy and in the unique power of the American democracy to improve the lives and the fortunes of all its citizens. He never allowed his position or his authority to separate him from those who lacked position and authority. He knew that "The rank is but the guinea's stamp." "A man's a man for a' that!"

And, I am also confident that his being a life-long Southern Baptist gave substance and power to his essentially optimistic nature. Ultimately, I think he knew no other faith than the one in which his father and mother and the churches of Oklahoma nurtured him. He rejoiced in the heritage of Wake Forest, he was sad when changing perspectives in the denomination caused it to become diminished, but he stood true to a vision of education that is morally and spiritually redemptive and that is rooted deeply in Baptist life.

I have said that Dr. Scales's nature was optimistic, and I think that it was. But this optimism was often and sorely tested. Many of us here today remember, with a grief that is still alive, the death of his talented and vivacious daughter Laura when she was a mere twenty years old. We also have unfading memories of his wife Betty Randel Scales, a woman of dignity and grace who filled every role she played –

teacher, mother, friend, First Lady of Wake Forest – with straightforward and unpretentious wisdom. And we have watched with admiration as Dr. Scales himself, sometimes alone on long nights and difficult days in the hospital, faced pain and death and, again and again, emerged victorious – ready once more to come back to work, to fly to Oklahoma, to take a Caribbean cruise, or just to go to a movie or read another book or visit another friend.

The Scales family (Laura, Betty, James Ralph, and Ann) in Rome, Italy

In this congregation I must speak also of the fourth member of the Scales family: Dr. Scales's second daughter, Ann, a woman well designed to enlarge the legacy of the family and its contributions to true and fully inclusive democracy. She is independent and courageous: gifted with both her mother's sensibility and her father's zest for life. She is their true heir, and they took pride in all that she has achieved. And I must also salute a man of unmatched importance to Dr. Scales: Willie Hughes. More than a companion, more than just a friend, he walked with Dr. Scales through the valley of the shadow of death, and to him, especially, all of us who loved Dr. Scales will be forever grateful and admiring.

The last time I saw President Scales, he did not, I think, know that I was there. We could no longer talk to each other, nor could we even make gestures that could be understood. I had seen him before under similar conditions, and, because his spirit was so endlessly resilient, he had always somehow managed to come home. This time I realized I was saying good-bye.

"It seems a kind of indignity to [a] noble ... soul," Ralph Waldo Emerson wrote for the funeral services of his friend Henry David Thoreau, that "he should depart out of nature. ... But [my friend], at least," said Emerson, "is content. His soul was made for the noblest society; he had ... exhausted the capabilities of this world; wherever there is knowledge, wherever there is virtue, wherever there is beauty, he will find a home."

And so it is with our friend James Ralph Scales. The "noble heart" has, we know to our sorrow, indeed departed from among us. He had "exhausted the capabilities of this world." But we have confidence that "wherever there is knowledge, wherever there is virtue, wherever there is beauty, he will find a home."

18 March 1996

Mark Reece

Alumnus, Dean's Office
Received the Medallion of Merit in 1996

There are many of us here this morning – and I am one of them – who consider Mark Reece as fine a man as they have ever known. And they honor him for a life lived beautifully and well.

Why is this so? What was there about Mark Reece that made us admire him so much?

There was, of course, his career: thirty-two years of service to Wake Forest, from the placid fifties through the turbulent sixties and seventies down to the fast-changing eighties. And somehow – today – I picture him, most of all, as he was in the sixties: an endlessly busy and endlessly creative dean of men: young, smiling, patient, irresistibly friendly.

Being a dean in those years was not easy. Students were restless, seething, sometimes angry, inclined to protest against whatever displeased them. The campus atmosphere was unpredictable and mercurial, if not revolutionary. And it was the peculiar responsibility of Mark and his friend and colleague Lu Leake, in this uncertain environment, to maintain order and discipline.

And they did so. Largely through the efforts of Mark and Lu, Wake Forest remained essentially unscarred. What happened in so many other places did not happen here – partly, I think, because Mark believed in the integrity of his assignment. He was a man of tradition, a family man, a church-going Baptist by inheritance and by conviction, and disrespect for propriety and law displeased him. He did not hesitate to stand ready outside a dormitory when disruption of the peace was threatened or to rebuke, and punish, a student who did violence to his – and Wake Forest's – convictions of what was right.

But there was another side to the sixties – and another side to Mark Reece. Beyond what was distasteful or threatening about those years, there was also an idealism, a high-mindedness of spirit that manifested itself again and again in, for example, the civil rights movement, in a concern for the poor and the dispossessed, in the rediscovery of the common man. The culture of Wake Forest student life, like the culture of the American young, was richly visible and full of vitality, and Mark understood and appreciated that culture.

So it was that Mark, even while being true to his burdensome duties as Dean of Men, saw to it that Wake Forest embraced what was valuable and inspirational about the young men and women of these "changing" times. And so, in those days, we heard speakers who came in from everywhere – left, right, and center; and we listened in huge crowds – to Joan Baez and Simon and Garfunkel and Peter, Paul, and Mary; and we watched movies – every night, if we chose – in a film program that was recognized as being among the very best in the nation. With the help of one secretary and a handful of gifted students, Mark was a veritable one-man Student Union. And, besides everything else, he invented the brilliant idea that Wake Forest should build a collection of contemporary art out of the best works that New York City had to offer. Go when you can to the Reece Gallery in the Benson Center and see what that collection has become: look at its variety, its boldness, its artistic summary of the last thirty years of American life.

That collection of art is a legacy of Mark Reece, and it will continue to illuminate our lives. But Mark's real legacy is elsewhere.

The last time I saw Mark, I was visiting him in his bedroom, surrounded by paintings and drawings and posters that were full of color and power. He was, as you know, very frail: he could not stand, he could not

Mark Reece finds that being Dean of Men does not offer sufficient diplomatic immunity against "Bunker" Hill, infamous campus cop.

hear, he must have been endlessly frustrated and in almost constant pain. But his smile was ready, his handshake was warm, his mind was vigorous, and – most of all – there was still a light in his eyes, undimmed and honest. And it was a light that could only have shown out of love.

We loved Mark Reece, I think, because – quite simply – he was lovable and because he loved us. He loved his colleagues; he loved his neighbors; he loved students, even – maybe especially – those whom he had to discipline. Many people come and go and even spend years on a college campus, and they may come to be respected for one thing or another. But Mark is one of those rare college people who deserve – and receive – our abiding love.

Maybe love came easy to him because, in his family, he was surrounded by so much love. When I think of Shirley, his college sweetheart and his wife of many happy years, I remember the familiar words of the marriage ceremony. Were these words ever more appropriate than they are today as we think of Shirley and Mark? "To have and to hold from this day forward, for better for worse, for richer for poorer, in sickness and in health, to love and to cherish, till death us do part." And after Mark and Shirley come Mark Junior and John and Jordan and their wives and Lisa and her husband and ten splendid grandchildren: a legacy beyond money or power or fame; a legacy of honor and of a love that to this very day "believeth all things, hopeth all things, endureth all things."

Some years ago I was asked to speak at a retirement dinner for Mark. I said about him then that he was a man "without pretense and without malice," and I concluded with some lines from Shakespeare that I would like to quote again this morning. In his tribute to Brutus, the "noblest Roman" of them all, Marc Antony says:

His life was gentle, and the elements
So mix'd in him that Nature might stand up
And say to all the world, "This was a man!"

"Gentle" may seem to be a little word, and "man" is also a little word. But, as Shakespeare uses them at the end of the play and at the end of Brutus's life, he suggests harmony and reconciliation and being at peace with oneself.

Mark Reece was at peace with himself. He was "gentle." He was also a "man." In fact, Mark Reece was – is – will remain for us all – the dean of men.

May 15, 1997

Bob Dyer

Dean's Office, Religion Faculty
Received the Medallion of Merit in 1985

I CANNOT SAY WHAT A GOOD MAN is, but if I were asked to write a definition of a good man, I would begin by looking at the life of Bob Dyer.

Not because he knew the Bible and studied it; not because he was a thoughtful and persuasive minister; not because he taught religion with conviction and learning; not because he carried out his administrative assignments with honesty and justice – though all these things are true. Bob's goodness was of a different order, and it was rare, and it was unmatched by anyone I know.

For twenty-five years I worked with Bob Dyer in Reynolda Hall. We saw each other almost every day, we served together on committees, we went to meals together (if we were fortunate, the meal was prepared by Mary), we talked often and at length. And, in particular, I watched students as they came to see him. Some came because they needed advice: he gave it freely and wisely and sometimes with startling directness and candor. Some came because they were in trouble; he helped them to find a way out. Some came because they were lonely; he offered himself as a friend. Some came because they were black or Asian or from a foreign land; he told them he loved them. Some came because they were poor; he gave them money. Some came because they had no place to live; he gave them a room in his house. No one who came remained outside the embrace of his arms. The rest of us in the office were, I think, kind and helpful people too. But Bob was more than kind and helpful. He gave others his home, his heart, himself.

Just a few weeks ago several of us who had known and loved Bob for a long time gathered with him and Mary on the side porch of their home. Bob was weak, and he moved slowly, but he recalled happier days, and he remembered former students, and he told funny stories, and he laughed and smiled and was alert for life. And I remembered that a favorite poem of his was Tennyson's "Ulysses," and somehow now, as I look back to that porch and those friends, what Ulysses says in Tennyson's poem seems like what Bob Dyer might have said, so I close with a reading from Alfred Tennyson's "Ulysses."

Assistant Dean Robert Dyer shares his prize-winning roses with an admiring student.

17 April 2001

Archie Ammons

Alumnus, Poet

These remarks were given at a University ceremony in his memory.

WE ARE HERE TODAY TO REMEMBER and to honor Archie Ammons. We are especially pleased that Archie's wife Phyllis and his sister Vida – and other family members – are with us.

Yesterday afternoon, members of the English faculty named their lounge for Archie. A plaque was installed, and some of his poems were read in celebration. Tonight at Reynolda House at 8:00, Helen Vendler of Harvard University will give a lecture on his poetry, and there will be musical selections by pianist Clifton Matthews and by soprano Marilyn Taylor, who will sing Ammons poems set to music by Kenneth Frazelle.

This afternoon, here in Davis Chapel, we come not to interpret Archie's poetry or to try to define his legacy to literature or even (though several of his poems will be read) to consider him as a poet. Scholars and critics and students and ordinary readers will be engaged in that discovery for all the years to come. Rather, we will see him as a man who became our friend, and we will pay tribute to him with music and words we hope he would have wanted to hear.

Fifty-five years ago a young man of twenty – from the farmlands of Columbus County in eastern North Carolina – a Navy veteran – sat on the back row of an English classroom and listened – how patiently, I do not know – as others spoke. Already, we know now, words were taking shape in his mind, but they did not make their way into campus publications, and he chose as his college major not English, but biology. He was, he once said, an "invisible" student, but when he left Wake Forest he carried with him two lifelong treasures: a rare though unrecognized promise for poetry and a young woman, his Spanish teacher, who became his wife.

Decades later, Archie – no longer unrecognized, no longer " invisible" (except when he chose to be) – returned to Wake Forest to receive an honorary degree. He did not like institutional occasions of any kind, and so he chose not to march in the procession or even to sit on the platform but rather to loiter at some distance on the grass and wait until a signal was given – at which time he came forward to hear the citation and receive his hood. Successfully honored, he then immediately left the stage.

On another, later visit to Wake Forest, the University united to pay him homage with workshops, discussions, readings by other poets. At the end of a crowded day, eight or ten of us (including another poet from Cornell and a poet from Michigan) sat or stood in the playroom of our house and listened as Archie played old-fashioned country hymns on a century-old upright piano in need of tuning. And gradually we began to sing: "The Old Rugged Cross," "In the Garden," "Amazing Grace." Was this return to the remembered songs of his people the expected end of an academically sophisticated day? Probably not. But Charles Ives would have understood. And Thomas Hardy and William Carlos Williams also, I think, would have understood.

Among those in the playroom that night were Archie's eastern North Carolina friends, Shelby and Nin Stephenson. They know his land, and they share his memories, and they will sing two songs he loved. You heard Nick Bragg playing other hymn tunes as you entered the Chapel. Later, Teresa Radomski will sing a favorite popular song of Archie's from the Rodgers and Hammerstein musical, *Carousel*, which opened on Broadway the year Archie came home from the War.

On a college campus where rituals of pretension are in place and there are often conforming assumptions about intellect and taste, Archie was his own strikingly independent self. He did not altogether trust colleges or faculties, even at Wake Forest or Cornell. He was impatient at literary assemblies and suppers and parties, often in a hurry to go. Once, I remember, we drove to a dinner in the mountains; ten or fifteen minutes before we would have arrived, he said we had come far enough, and he turned around, and we went home. He liked to sit in the English department lounge and talk with other professors, and he was disappointed when nobody came by. He asked people how they were and what they were doing, and he listened attentively to what they said. On the day before he died, as my wife

Emily leaned over his bed to speak to him for the last time, she remembers that he said, "How's your mother?" When he went out to supper in Winston-Salem, he invariably picked the K&W Cafeteria – not Ryan's or Staley's or some restaurant that pride of position might have suggested. He did not burden himself with possessions, even books. His wants were few. He lived "deliberately" and "sturdily and Spartan-like" so as "to put to rout all that was not life."

That quotation from Thoreau reminds me of how profoundly American Archie was. He used to say to me, "Why is Wake Forest publishing Irish poetry?" and one night he gave a reading of Yeats's "The Wild Swans at Coole" that was so gleefully iconoclastic that, ever since, I have been almost embarrassed to teach it. He once received a traveling fellowship from the American Academy and went to Europe, but after only a few months he returned home, and he never went back. He would not fly in a plane. The one time, some years ago, he was in the air, he said that, if God let him survive, he would never get in another plane.

Archie once remarked that, if he were called upon to give his "last lecture," it would be on Ralph Waldo Emerson. He looked back to Emerson with a sympathy and a delight that he accorded few other writers of the past. And Emerson seemed to me to be looking ahead to Archie. When Emerson wrote to "The Poet" of the future, he said: "Thou shalt not know any longer the times, customs, graces, politics, or opinions of men, but shalt take all from the muse… And this is the reward; that the ideal shall be real to thee, and the impressions of the actual world shall fall like summer rain…Wherever snow falls or water flows or birds fly, wherever day and night meet in twilight, wherever the blue heaven is hung by clouds or sown with stars, wherever are forms with transparent boundaries, wherever are outlets into celestial space, wherever is danger, and awe, and love, – there is Beauty, plenteous as rain, shed for thee, and though thou shouldst walk the world over, thou shall not be able to find a condition inopportune or ignoble."

If I have stressed the simplicity of Archie's outward life, it is to sharpen our awareness of the subtlety of his inner life, the intricacy of his language, and the complexity of his artistic vision. Future readers will know Archie only as a poet, and they will rejoice and prosper. We know him as a poet too, and we are grateful, but we also knew him as a friend, and if he had never written a line of verse, we would have watched him, listened to him, and loved him. "The private life of one man," Emerson wrote, is "a more illustrious monarchy… more sweet and serene in its influence to its friend, than any kingdom in history." We have been blessed by Archie's influence on us all, and we give thanks.

April 19, 2001

Dolly McPherson

English Faculty

"WE WOULD LIKE FOR YOU TO TALK about Dolly McPherson," they said. "Good," I said. "I'd like to." "You have three minutes!" they said. "Three minutes," I thought to myself. Why, I could spend three minutes admiring the colorful flowers she so tenderly nurtures in front of her apartment. And another three minutes just glancing at her art collection. And another three minutes – no, make that a half-hour – remembering delicious – and inimitable – food from her kitchen.

And I haven't even mentioned her singing and her laughter, still echoing down the corridors of my memory. And her infectious enthusiasm for the sheer pleasure of living, even when she is in pain. And her cheerful presence in an academic department too often quiet and – let's admit it – rather too staid and serious.

And I begin to realize that half my time has gone by, and I haven't even spoken about her teaching: how, with her inspirational love of literature and her exacting standards, she has led students through texts both familiar and new and brought them to an appreciation of insights and points of view that, on this conventional campus, they might otherwise have never experienced.

And, beyond my allotted time, I could, as the popular song says, "write a book" about her place in Wake Forest history: how she came, twenty-seven years ago, as a happy and courageous pioneer, the first in a line – still far too short a line – of women and men who have challenged our historic assumptions about race and culture. And how much richer and wiser we are because she did come!

Since I was given only three minutes, I can explore no further. So, with just a few seconds left, I must sum up what might otherwise have been an extended tribute and declare my gratitude – and the gratitude of my wife Emily and my three children – to Dolly for having pointed the way to a more unclouded future for us all – and also offer our enduring love to one whom we are proud to call our dear friend.

May 11, 2001

Bill Starling
Alumnus, Dean of Admissions

I DO NOT KNOW OF ANY LIFE STORY in the annals of Wake Forest that compares – in lifelong commitment, in selfless dedication, in wholesome influence – with Bill Starling's. How can even those of us who knew him best – even those who worked with him every day – begin to count and to consider the thousands of young college-bound men and women whom he, with a welcome and a handshake, met and then patiently listened to and wisely counseled? Their numbers are beyond our reckoning. And what was uniquely remarkable about Bill was that the high school student who came expectantly to his office last week saw, when he looked into Bill's face, the same smiling, enthusiastic, youthful person seen by that first prospective Wake Forest student – by now, perhaps, a grandparent – who had Bill's first admissions appointment in 1958 – forty-three years ago.

Even those of us who applauded the selection of Bill as Director of Admissions on that long-ago day could not have foreseen that he was destined to have a career unparalleled, as far as I know, in American colleges and universities. Even Dean Bill Archie, who, with little more than intuition but with uncannily accurate vision, picked Bill out of the class of 1957, could not have known the ultimate wisdom of his choice. We knew that Bill was a leader: in his fraternity and in student government he had been elected to high office, and he was both respected and popular. We knew that he was smart: I had taught him in four English courses, and each time he had made an A – in a field not his own.

But Bill was more than smart or talented. He did not parade his intellect or lead by commandment. Rather, he had a quiet confidence that he could do what had to be done, and that confidence never left him. He was shrewd in his judgments and fair in giving voice to them, and in his work and in his life he was incorruptible. He knew who he was, and that self-knowledge gave him strength to succeed and, in William Faulkner's great words, to "endure and prevail."

We will not honor Bill if today we praise him and tomorrow we forsake his legacy. We too, like Bill, must have faith: faith in our calling and in the useful possibilities of every day and every conversation. And we must have hope: hope for the young, however unpromising or immature they might be. And every decision we make about another human being must, if possible, be sprinkled by love. For faith is more important than rank. And hope is more important than statistics. And love is more important than achievement. Those convictions are at the foundation of Wake Forest and are what have made Wake Forest – at its best and noblest – a place worthy of our service and our affection.

For Bill truly loved Wake Forest, and he loved his friends: those who worked with him, those who used to work with him, those whom he remembered from bygone days, those whom he played golf with or went to the beach with, old friends from Smithfield, newer friends from across the nation who, one day in his office, were touched by the interest he took in them.

And, most of all, he loved his family. Elinor, his hometown bride of forty-four years, devoted and calm and still beautiful. His daughter Jennie. His son Gray. His brother Mike. And his four grandchildren: Rebecca, Benjamin, Elizabeth and Virginia. I think there was not a time during these last few years, when Bill and I talked, that the conversation did not turn to his grandchildren. Because of them and because of Elinor and Jennie and Gray, he looked ahead joyfully to years of retirement.

And now we know that those years will not come, and we are saddened – and we grieve – in a way that defies easy consolation. (Certainly, no words from a mere layman like me can suffice to explain or to justify or to wipe away tears.) The poet Yeats, reacting to the sudden death of a young and "dear" friend, said that, although he had become "accustomed" to the fact of eventual death, he could not believe that this young man he so much admired and loved could "share" in what he called the "discourtesy of death." Similarly, death came discourteously – without warning – to Bill, and we are heart-broken.

This afternoon, in talking about Bill, I have often used the word "young." But, after all, Bill was 65, and he was a grandfather. And yet the word "young" is right, I think, and perhaps it is in stressing that word "young" that we can better understand what happened to Bill four days ago. Maybe, in some providential way, Bill was not meant to grow old.

Maybe we will be strangely blessed to be able always to see him as busy, active, talkative, cheerful, forward-looking, amused about life, and therefore truly "young." We can always see that boyish look he had when he crinkled his eyes and smiled.

The first time I met Bill, I think, he was sitting at a counter in Dick Frye's restaurant in old Wake Forest, having supper. He was 18 and a new freshman, and I introduced myself and said, "Welcome to Wake Forest." "Welcome to Wake Forest!" How many times in after years must Bill have said those same words to an eighteen-year-old student? And how appropriate and right it was that the words came from Bill – because, as if in defiance of time, Bill was – somehow – to the last – still eighteen years old himself.

He who binds to himself a joy
Does the winged life destroy;
But he who kisses the joy as it flies
Lives in eternity's sun rise.*

Welcome to the sunrise, Bill!

June 22, 2001

*These lines of poetry are from William Blake.

Bynum Shaw

Alumnus, Journalism Faculty

THE AUTUMN OF 1946 on the Wake Forest College campus – the "old" campus – was a season of gratitude and promise – of "mellow fruitfulness," to use the poet Keats's words. Young men had returned home from around the world, exhilarated by victories overseas and confident about the nation's future and about their own. They gathered in clusters of relaxed and eager friendship – not so much to remember as to celebrate: to read, to write, to learn, to savor meals together, to go to an occasional movie or bridge game or football contest or party, sometimes simply to enjoy "unprofitable talk at morning hours."

I was in one such group of friends. Our favorite meeting places were Miss Jo Williams' cafeteria, the booths outside the College Book Store, the Alumni Building, and – especially – the student publications offices on what we called "Pub Row." Bynum Shaw was in that group: immensely talented, witty, wise beyond his years, and unceasingly kind to us all. He had come to Wake Forest in 1940, bringing with him success and recognition as a skillful and articulate high school debater, but he had left college early to volunteer for wartime service in the Merchant Marine – he loved the ocean – and had returned to Wake Forest that fall to finish his degree. An intelligent and thoughtful use of words – spoken or written – was always at the center of Bynum's life, and in the undergraduate years that remained he seized so fully whatever opportunities for writing came his way that Dr. Edgar Folk, the journalism mentor of us all, began to identify Bynum as the one person he most wanted to succeed him some day on the faculty at Wake Forest.

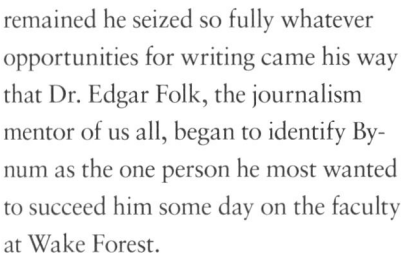

What happened after 1948 is a story of remarkable growth and achievement. In his newspaper assignments, notably on the *Baltimore Sun* – as city reporter, as editorial writer, as overseas correspondent – he was piercingly keen in his insights, sound in his judgments, and eminently fair and honest. He considered journalism a noble profession, and he brought to it his own native nobility. He also found in the post-War Germany of his years with the *Baltimore Sun* the themes and characters and narrative excitement of his first two novels: *The Sound of Small Hammers* and *The Nazi Hunter*.

In 1965 Bynum, as expected, came back "home" to take Dr. Folk's place in the classroom and as adviser to student publications. Like his predecessor, he emphasized learning in the liberal arts rather than technical skill, and he encouraged his students to take courses in literature, history, political science, and economics. Needless to say, he was happy to be in the English department, and he excelled in his new career: he was the first Wake Forest professor to receive the Jon Reinhardt Award for excellence in teaching.

I could say more about Bynum as a writer and a teacher. I could mention the two other novels that he wrote. I could speak at length and admiringly of his history of Wake Forest for the years from 1943 to 1967: carefully researched, crowded with events and people, highly readable.

And I could recount the testimony of former students who valued his judgments and have been faithful to his ideals, largely because they saw him as a man worth following. As one alumnus said in a recent letter to Bynum, "You stirred the passion for the profession in my soul." And another wrote, "I could never repay you for the gift" you gave me.

But Bynum's books are on library shelves, and his students – some of them here today – can – and will, I am sure – speak for themselves. I want to talk about another Bynum Shaw: the man beyond – or inside – the writer and the teacher: a man with a capacity for friendship such as I have seldom known. A man who, in travel and change, never forgot his friends. A man who, for example, years after they had separated, brought some of these friends together on a Maryland lawn to eat North Carolina barbecue. A man who opened his door, in transparently happy welcome, to whoever came to visit. A man who, in retirement himself, regularly assembled other retired faculty and staff members for meals and conversation: a generous idea that only Bynum, it seems, could have envisioned and carried out. A man who was at the center of a circle of appreciation and concern.

This has been a sad year for Wake Forest, and today I think not only of Bynum Shaw but also of Bob Dyer and Archie Ammons and Bill Starling and Elizabeth Jones Brantley. How much we have lost in just a few months! And what I will miss is not so much their skills and talents, their success in life, as their goodness, their decency, their humanity, their very presence.

Sometimes I "despair that time" may not bring "that selfsame excellence again." But I do find consolation in realizing that all these friends were shaped, at least in part, by Wake Forest and that those shaping powers and ideals are still around us – if we can only recognize them and believe in them as Bynum Shaw and the others did.

Quite by coincidence, a few weeks ago I was reading a play by the distinguished dramatist August Wilson called *Joe Turner's Come and Gone.* One of the characters talks about what he calls the Secret of Life. A person can discover the Secret of Life, he says, by first finding the one song he has been destined to sing. If he finds that song, he can lie down at the end of his life and "die a happy man": a man who has "left his mark on life."

The character who is speaking says that he has found his song. It is the Binding Song. I take the power of the song, he says, and I bind people together. I've been "binding people" together ever since I found my song. "Just like glue" I stick people together. (And here is what is so remarkably appropriate for today.) "That's why," the man says, "they call me Bynum. I bind people together."

Like the fictional Bynum, our friend Bynum long ago found his song, and he sang it all his life – in Bath, in Wilmington, in "old" Wake Forest, in the North Atlantic, in Baltimore, in Germany, at Worrell House in London, and here in Winston-Salem, surrounded by Charlotte and Bonnie and Susan and his grandchildren and by the sweet memories of those other men and women of his past who knew him and loved him. Having found his song, our Bynum did indeed leave his mark on life – and on all of us who called him "friend."

"Blest be the tie that binds."

August 30, 2001

Jack Nowell
Alumnus, Chemistry Faculty

No one of us here this afternoon, I can safely assume, could have known the first Professor of Chemistry at Wake Forest to be named John William Nowell. That Dr. Nowell was graduated from the College in 1903 and, after receiving his Ph.D. from Johns Hopkins, returned to teach on the old campus until his death in 1930. "He carried into his lecture room and laboratory," one of his colleagues said of him, "the high ideals and demands of modern scholarship, and yet his quiet and strong example as a man among men was the force that won him the love and devotion of all students who filled his classroom."

This Professor Nowell was, of course, our friend Jack's father, and he died when Jack was only ten. Whether from inheritance, or lessons learned from his father at home, or hours spent in Lea Laboratory, or tales told by other teachers who lived up and down Faculty Avenue, the son absorbed the father's reputation and chose to follow in his footsteps. The pattern was the same: an undergraduate degree from Wake Forest, a Ph.D. in chemistry, and – for Jack, in 1945 – an appointment to the Wake Forest faculty. The rest of the story we know, for it describes his life among us as a scientist teacher, his leadership on the faculty, his unfailing dedication to his alma mater, and the gift of loyal friendship which he bestowed so generously across our campus and across our community.

Jack taught chemistry for forty-two years, eleven of them before the College moved to Winston-Salem. Almost every student on the "old campus" who studied chemistry or who hoped for a career in medicine or academic scholarship knew Jack. Like other faculty members of those days he taught long hours, served on numerous committees, advised and counseled and was always available. He must have said "yes" to every request anyone ever made for help.

His home was only a few minutes away from his laboratory, and the College and the College town were entwined gently into each other.

But, when the historic move to a new campus came, Jack – as I recall – went willingly and with a sense of challenge. Though devoted to the symbols of his past, he was never unrealistically sentimental, and Winston-Salem offered a brand-new science building and enlarged facilities and opportunities. So Jack said goodbye to Lea Laboratory and set his face toward Salem Hall, where, as the next three decades went by, his administrative talents led him into the chairmanship of the Department and where, with the support of a few equally determined and committed colleagues, he helped define and establish Master's and Ph.D. programs in chemistry. By the time of Jack's retirement, the Department's future was assured and destined to be strong.

Jack was able, I think, to lead Chemistry to an enlarged vision of itself not only because he knew his subject but because, in so many other ways, his mind was quick and alert and disciplined. His head was filled with information. We used to say of Jack that, whatever subject came up for discussion, he knew something about it. I have met few people who were blessed with such wide-ranging intellectual curiosity or such an all-encompassing memory. Facts, faces, experiences, things read or seen – once having entered his mind – stayed there. A conversation with Jack was an introduction to his thoughts that could lead you almost anywhere.

I have said that Jack's mind was alert and his memory keen. I became aware of this whenever I played bridge with Jack, always hoping that I would be his partner rather than his opponent. He not only remembered every card that had been played in a given hand and who had played it; at the end of the evening he could recount, card by card, what had happened hours earlier. He could even recall especially memorable hands from the past, when so-and-so, for example, had an Ace, King, and Jack of Hearts and he had a Queen, 10, 9, 6, and 4, and he had won. (I am told that his mind was equally agile and fact-filled when it came to the stock market.)

Jack liked to entertain friends. No married couple's home could surpass in taste or elegance a meal that Jack could prepare in his bachelor quarters. Every dish was planned with care, served in style, and eaten to the accompaniment of generosity and thoughtfulness. I seldom saw Jack more content with life than when he was surrounded at supper by men and women whom he had chosen to be his friends.

From right: Chemistry Professors Nowell, Gross, Isbell, Furman and Miller

It is good this afternoon that we can look back on Jack's life and remember him when he was active and well and keen-spirited and eager for learning and for company. For that is the true Jack Nowell, the good man who was our good friend. In recent years, as we all know, ill health had taken away the sparkle and enthusiasm that were his natural charms, but I like to think that he continued to remember us as we remember him, and I was comforted to learn that, not many nights ago, he asked to be taken outdoors to see the meteor shower that was coming into our skies. As he looked up toward the heavens, he might well have seen, as far as we know, more than the rest of us would have seen. If so, he was simply being his old self: the same boy who, a long time ago, first looked into a chemistry laboratory and wondered what secrets lay there, waiting to be discovered.

November 20, 2001

Russell Brantley
Alumnus, Director of the News Bureau

Received the Medallion of Merit in 1987

IF HEMINGWAY OR Scott Fitzgerald or Thomas Wolfe had wandered onto the Wake Forest campus of the mid-1940's – in body or in spirit – and had made his way to the offices of *Old Gold and Black*, *The Student*, and *The Howler*, he would – at almost any hour of the night or day, by the light of the sun or by the light of the moon – have found congenial company. The little publications rooms – with their well-worn typewriters and their scarred desks – would have been crowded with aspiring writers, captivated – indeed, almost overwhelmed – by a fascination with words: words, as Dylan Thomas said, that "tick" and "beat" and "blaze." The visitor would have met students ambitious that they too might some day write a novel, or maybe a few poems or short stories, that would be noticed and talked about.

For, indeed, the Wake Forest campus then was a haven for young men – and a handful of young women – who read books greedily and wrote with hope and passion. The student newspaper did – truly – "cover the campus like the magnolias," and conversations among these students almost always turned to "What books have you read lately?" and "What are you writing now?" Sometimes the students would drift downtown to Shorty's or – once in a while – find a car or truck and go to Josh Turnage's in Durham, where unlimited barbecue and unlimited beer were always available for little more than a dollar and a song. And sometimes – whenever mere conversation lagged, as it rarely but sometimes did – the students did sing.

One of the few young women who graced the student publications world was a faculty daughter named Elizabeth Jones: pretty, smart, modest and shy. Her father had taught English at Wake Forest for twenty-some years, and she was immersed in the school's culture. The young man who became her best friend and later her husband was a lively, boyish, still unfinished fellow named Russell Brantley: fresh from a small town in eastern North Carolina and, like the best of his contemporaries, eager to see his name in print.

So it was that Russell and Lib met, not knowing that, even before the College moved to Winston-Salem, they would come back to Wake Forest to live out their productive lives and to raise three children who, like them, would find challenge and promise in words. In this very chapel we have mourned their son Russ, and just a few years ago we remembered and mourned Lib. I know that Robin and Ben – and Carter and Anna too – understand how central to the story of Wake Forest are our memories of Russ and Lib – and now, our memories of Russell himself.

Russell never gave up his ambition to be a better and better writer. Even in his last years he was working on a novel which gave promise, many of us thought, of being his crowning achievement. And his energy never flagged. He remained endlessly youthful – in his looks, in his quick observations of the world around him, in his enthusiasm, in his friendship for others. I recall his gleeful satisfaction when *Fetch Life*, his book of poems, appeared, and he was invited to read aloud from it at local gatherings. And he never ceased to be remembered as the author of that controversial Baptist story *The Education of Jonathan Beam*.

Russell and Lib Brantley

But Russell's rare talent for seeing and understanding and interpreting life carried him also in a different direction: a direction that would not have been foreseen by someone like me who knew him when he was a brash twenty-year-old. For he always had about him a happy touch of anti-establishment irony and sarcasm, and he could – and often did – adopt the guise of a knowing cynic. He was also – rightly – suspicious of institutions, even his alma mater when he thought that it had betrayed the best part of itself. Yet for most of his life, as it turned out, he placed his gifts with words at the service of an institution – this institution – and it was his singular responsibility to defend it when it came under attack and to criticize it when it was untrue to what he saw as its most enduring ideals. Each of the three presidents for whom he worked knew what it was to be given new strength and encouragement by Russell, and each of them also felt the honest power of his disagreements. Instead of being compelled always to promote the public relations image that the University had determined for itself, he remained strangely independent and, when necessary, courageously candid.

Partly because of his forthrightness and honesty, Russell was a good companion. For fifty years or more I was his friend. We gave each other support and counsel. We reminisced about the old campus and our schoolboy days there, we went on barbecue expeditions, we exchanged books that we liked, we talked endlessly about Wake Forest and about Wake Forest men and women we had known, we remembered moments – both high and low – in our lives. Russell always listened intently to what I – and others – were saying, and he invariably noticed what was going on around him. Conversations with him were genuinely shared, and they were intense. There was no one else quite like him. In Wake Forest history he – somehow – stands alone: a central figure in the Wake Forest myth: part fact, part legend.

During the last several years Russell and I have gone to lunch every few weeks. The pattern has always been the same. I have picked him up at his home about 12:15, and we have headed for Noble's, where each of us has ordered a fried oyster salad – the only question for us has been whether we should ask for six oysters or for nine – and then, for dessert, bread pudding. Only last month we followed the same luncheon ritual. He seemed relaxed and content with life. I did not know it would be our last lunch together. I am not sure that I will ever order a fried oyster salad again.

So, we'll go no more a roving
   So late into the night,
Though the heart be still as loving,
   And the moon be still as bright.

For the sword outwears its sheath,
And the soul wears out the breast,
   And the heart must pause to breathe,
And love itself have rest.

[So] we'll go no more a roving
*By the light of the moon.**

February 16, 2005

*These lines of poetry are from Lord Byron.

Marjorie Crisp

Physical Education Faculty

TODAY WE REMEMBER – gratefully and with admiration – a true Wake Forest pioneer, a pathfinder upon whose strong shoulders the structures and the achievements of Wake Forest women's athletics were built and nourished. If today we point with pride to competitive women's teams, to award-winning women athletes, even – yes – to national championships in women's sports, we must acknowledge that in Marge Crisp's talents and dedication – and in her heart – we find the origins of our triumphs.

Wake Forest had been coeducational for only five years when Marge Crisp arrived in 1947 to become the first "Instructor in Physical Education for Women." Only about seventeen per cent of the student body were female, and Marge, I guess, taught and knew them all. She also began to develop an intramural program for women students, and in 1949 she was joined by another physical education instructor, Dorothy Casey, her lifelong collaborator and friend. Crisp and Casey: these names were to resound for decades – and still resound – in the story of Wake Forest.

Advances were slow in coming: money was scarce, and men's programs quickly swallowed up whatever funds were available. But Marge persevered. She was good at waiting. She never stopped pushing, she never gave up, but she was tactful and diplomatic, and her talents – and her graciousness and good will in using her talents – were destined, year by year, to bring her success. In 1967 she became Director of Physical Education for Women, working side by side with the esteemed gentleman chairman Harold Barrow, and in 1971 she was named director of women's athletics (again a "first" in Wake Forest history), working with Gene Hooks, another legendary Wake Forest athletics professional.

Marge's first annual budget for her entire program was $500, and I have heard stories about how she counted every penny before spending it and also about how she used her own money to buy meals for students when the University could not – or would not – provide it. She was also – for thirteen years – the women's golf coach. Season after season, bit by bit, women's programs became more widely recognized, and by the time she retired, the foundation had been laid, and it was a foundation of honor and character and academic achievement that was a counterpoint to the athletic skills that the young women brought to the games and matches they played.

Marge's retirement years were years of continuing honors and recognitions, and she enjoyed the warm friendships of the colleagues she had worked with and the students she had taught. She played golf, of course, and she took pleasure in the programs of the Senior Ladies Golf Association, now called the "Marge Crisp Invitational." I am told that she delighted in card games, and – from what I have heard – I am glad that I never had to face a challenge from her across a card table. Her Christmas parties were a source of delight to all who came, and she never lost her enthusiasm for Wake Forest and for Wake Forest athletics, men's as well as women's. Wherever Deacons gathered, she was toasted and loved.

In our modern university, well endowed and well equipped and widely known and praised, we are fortunate beyond our dreams of earlier years. We can – with satisfaction – look at Wake Forest and applaud what we see and be thankful. But somehow I think that, if Marge Crisp were with us today – and maybe if she could be joined by "Skeeter" Francis and Pat Preston and Russell Brantley and others whom we have recently lost – not to mention others still with us whom I see within this congregation this afternoon – they would say that nothing was more glorious than those years of early struggle when – with almost no staff support, against odds, without resources, and with little publicity – so much was accomplished with so little. It is harder to be a pioneer, to find new trails and to make new paths, than to walk well-trodden paths; it is more difficult to build a house than to live in a house built by others. But if you are a pioneer – then, in your heart, and with all the strength of your spirit, you know with gratefulness where it was you came from and what you did, and you can be thrilled to look around you and say, "It is good." Marge Crisp was such a pioneer; she could look today at women's athletics at Wake Forest and say, "It is good." And we who are her friends can say back to her, "You were the first among those who made it so."

February 16, 2005

Bashir El-Beshti

English Faculty

An English department – perhaps more than any other department (though perhaps I am simply revealing my own bias when I say so) – is (or should be) a place of welcome, a home to good will, an oasis in a troubled world where men and women can gather in openness and honesty and, most of all, in friendship – to teach and to learn and, if fortune blesses them, to become more wise.

I hope that Bashir found our English department here at Wake Forest such a place. I believe that he did – in large part because he brought to it the very qualities I mention. Coming to us – fifteen years ago – from a land and a culture we did not really know, he was able to tell us about Orientalism, about Islam, and about postcolonial literature, and he – alone among us – could teach literary Arabic. In Shakespeare and in Renaissance drama he found sources of especially appropriate inspiration, and I note, among his publications, articles on Marlowe's *Tamburlaine* and on "Shakespeare and the Fashioning of an Arab State."

I think, however, that we his colleagues – and, maybe also his students – will remember Bashir less for what he taught and for what he wrote than for who he was. At the services in the Muslim Cemetery on Sunday, as I summoned up favorite images of Bashir, two passages from Shakespeare came forcefully into my mind. One from *Julius Caesar*: "His life was gentle." Another, from *Henry V*: "A good leg will fall, a straight back will stoop, …a fair face will wither, …but a good heart …is the sun and the moon; or rather, the sun, and not the moon, for it shines bright and never changes, but keeps his course truly." The first passage is about Brutus, "the noblest Roman of them all," and the second is said by Henry about himself, but the words none the less describe the Bashir El-Beshti I knew: "His life was gentle." He had "a good heart." And he kept "his course truly."

I believe that a memorial like this one today, though we are here, first of all, to celebrate a man we knew and loved, is also an occasion for us to look at ourselves and at the department and college we represent. We are living in a world which divides and saddens and terrifies us and which, far too often, creates enemies rather than friends. Let us, in memory of Bashir, be "gentle" and keep our "course truly" and be to one another like brothers and sisters and create, at least in miniature, the kind of world we would most like to live in.

More than a century ago, Walt Whitman prophesied such a world: one in which

All affection shall be fully responded to
– the secret shall be told;
All these separations and gaps shall be taken up,
and hook'd and link'd together;
The whole Earth – this cold, impassive, voiceless Earth,
shall be completely justified;
…
…the vast…globe, given, and giving all,
Europe to Asia, Africa join'd, and they to the New World;
The lands, geographies, dancing before you,
holding a festival garland,
As brides and bridegrooms hand in hand.

March 24, 2005

B. G. Gokhale
Asian Studies Faculty

THE YEAR IS 1960. At Wake Forest, as on most American college campuses, words like "international" and "global" and "multicultural" were not yet part of the every-day academic vocabulary. Travel abroad was an opportunity enjoyed only by the favored few. The College catalog showed no awareness of the world east and south of Europe – unless one counts an occasional course like "World Religions" or "The British Empire."

Fortunately for Wake Forest, a far-seeing administrator, William C. Archie, had been, for two brief years, Dean of the College, and he had set in motion a plan to develop at Wake Forest a program in Asian studies, with a concentration on South Asia. His idea received necessary financial support from the Mary Reynolds Babcock Foundation, and a search was at once underway for a scholar who would direct the program.

Few faculty searches at Wake Forest have been as successful as the one that found Balkrishna (B.G.) Gokhale and brought him to this campus. Though only forty-one years old, he was already the author of five books – *The Making of the Indian Nation* and *Indian Thought through the Ages*, to name only two. He had taught in Bombay and, in this country, at Bowdoin College and at Oberlin College, and at the time of his appointment here he was on the faculty at the University of Washington.

So, when Dr. Gokhale arrived in Winston-Salem in 1960, we knew that we had among us – for the first time in our history – a true Asian scholar, a man – from elsewhere, so to speak – who could introduce us to a world about which we knew so little. And during all the years after 1960 he continued – honorably and indefatigably – his career in research, writing twelve more books as well as articles for journals all around the world. Look at the Gokhale shelf in the Library, and you'll see what I mean.

Dr. Gokhale's teaching also remained central to his life: for undergraduates, such courses as the "History and Civilization of Southeast Asia" and "Modern India"; for graduate students, seminars on India and Southeast Asia; and later, courses in elementary and intermediate Hindi. Always eager to tell others about the culture of his native country, he constantly modified and enlarged his own understanding of his discipline. He seemed never to rest from his labors.

In 1970 Dr. Gokhale took a group of twenty students abroad for a semester in India. They studied at Fergusson College in Poona, and for three weeks they toured India and Nepal. This venture overseas came before the Wake Forest house in Venice opened and before Worrell House in London was even thought of – and decades, of course, before going to some other place in the world became part of the education of so many of our students of today.

B.G. and Beena Gokhale

All the while he was writing and teaching; Dr. Gokhale was active among us, his colleagues and his neighbors, in introducing us, too, to the civilization, the philosophy, the art, the religion of his homeland. How many times have I been with him and his beloved wife Beena, and how much I have learned about their traditions and their values and their expectations from life, and, I must say too, how happily I have partaken of the dishes of food served at Mrs. Gokhale's dinners

Edwin G. Wilson | 73

and receptions. She is an incomparable hostess, a devoted wife and mother, and a charming and gracious woman who, in her own less public way, willingly shared with us her insights and her talents.

Professor Gokhale was frequently asked to discuss his specialty by various campus organizations.

Under the encouraging influence of Dr. Gokhale, others on the Wake Forest faculty, much more than I, began learning about Asia, developed new courses themselves, and, sometimes at faculty gatherings, read papers on Asian-related subjects they had become interested in. Throughout the 1960s and 1970s, in particular, Wake Forest was alive with an awareness of Asia – an awareness that was heightened by visitors like Dr. and Mrs. Htin Aung from Burma; another Indian scholar, Amiya Chakravarty; and the great Ravi Shankar, all of them here primarily because of the Asian Studies program that Dr. Gokhale had initiated in 1960.

I hope it is all right to quote myself from another occasion when I said to an alumni Homecoming group that Wake Forest should always "stand up" for humanity "in all its diversity and richness," and be "a place of learning which men and women of good will everywhere might, if they knew it, be happy to call home."

I think that Dr. Gokhale was truly happy to call Wake Forest "home," and Wake Forest is a better and richer place because he did call it "home." We are grateful for his career but, perhaps even more, for his friendship, and we say today to his wife and his two gifted daughters how much we treasure our continuing memories of his forty-five years in our lives.

In conclusion I would like to read a few passages from an eminent poet of India, the Nobel Laureate Rabindranath Tagore.

I have had my invitation to this world's festival and thus my life has been blessed. My eyes have seen and my ears have heard.

I have tasted of the hidden honey of this lotus that expands on the ocean of light, and thus am I blessed…

We were neighbours for long… Now the day has dawned and the lamp that lit my dark corner is out. A summons has come and I am ready for my journey.

At this time of my parting, wish me good luck, my friends! The sky is flushed with the dawn and my path lies beautiful. I start on my journey with [an] expectant heart.

No more sailing from harbor to harbor…

Into the audience hall where swells up the music of toneless strings I shall take this harp of my life. I shall tune it to the notes of forever and lay down my silent harp…

August 16, 2005

Charles Allen

Alumnus, Biology Faculty
Received the Medallion of Merit in 1976

FOR TWO-THIRDS OF A CENTURY Charles Allen gave his mind, his heart, and – when necessary – his muscle to the college he loved. And by means of that constant and unfailing loyalty he helped to define the special character – and the central paradox – of Wake Forest and to give Wake Forest a purpose and an outlook uniquely its own. A church-going Southern Baptist, he, like his teacher and mentor William Louis Poteat, taught evolution; a meticulous and exacting scientist, he reserved his greatest passion for classical music; respectful of tradition, he admired the shapes and forms of modern art; a small-town Southern boy, he worked to tear down the barriers that here in our homeland we had erected to separate people from each other. Surely, the Wake Forest of today is blessed that in years of great change – for the country and for the University – people like Charlie Allen were here with us to remind us of our honored past and to illustrate by example how the best of that past can be incorporated into our future – without any sacrifice of its essence.

My own friendship with Charlie goes all the way back to the fall of 1942: to a house on Faculty Avenue in the town of Wake Forest: a house owned by Mrs. Fannie Gorrell (a daughter of President Charles Taylor and the widow of a German professor) where Charlie and I had upstairs rooms. He was already teaching biology, of which I knew little, and I was a College senior who had been named editor of the yearbook, *The Howler*. One of Charlie's many talents was in photography, and he volunteered to take pictures of the signature old campus buildings for inclusion – full page – in the yearbook. He took the pictures, and I still have them: still authentic, still true, still (for an older campus alumnus) able to stir sweet memories. (Incidentally, I first met Clara on the front porch of Mrs. Gorrell's house; she had come up for a visit with Charlie.)

This experience was my introduction to the versatility of Charlie Allen: a versatility so pronounced and so rare that legend – legend based on fact – has many times labeled him a "Renaissance man." And his long career at Wake Forest only enlarged and intensified our awareness of how much he deserved that title. Whom has this University known – whom have we seen – who with such apparent ease and such impeccable taste mastered so many skills of hand and ear and eye?

I never took a biology course and must therefore keep my silence on that subject. (I do know from others what a dedicated and inspirational teacher he was.) But almost every day I walk or drive by Winston Hall and I look not only at that building but across the grassy fields to the Scales Fine Arts Center – for me not only the most original but the most beautifully and most intricately designed building on our campus – and I remember that every day of construction Charlie was there: watching, supervising, insisting on quality. We used to say that not a brick went into place without his approval. The Center is a monument to him as well as to the President for whom it is named.

And who among us – of sufficient age – can forget those glorious evenings in Wait Chapel when we heard the world's greatest performers – selected and brought here by Charlie Allen during his nineteen years as Director of the Artist Series? Rubinstein, Menuhin, Marian Anderson, Leontyne Price, Schwarzkopf and Nilsson, the New York Philharmonic, the London Symphony, the Moscow Chamber Orchestra, and on and on. So magnificent were the setting and the sound we might well have thought ourselves in New York or London or Paris.

I suppose that in part Charlie acquired his matchless understanding of music from his enormous record collection, but we must not overlook his comparably matchless wife Clara, a singer of grace and beauty. In the years when they lived on Faculty Drive they together set a standard – in yard, in garden, in interior rooms, in decor, and yes, in food – that was the envy of visitors like me. Everything one saw had its own integrity.

Charlie was a man of strong opinions, and he never hesitated – in faculty meetings, in committees, in private conversations, in speaking to administrators, as I well know – to express those opinions and to say – or at least to imply – that those who did not agree with him were either ignorant or misinformed. He was not modest or shy. But at the same time he was able to look beyond any moment of uneasiness or dispute or prideful argument to what he saw as the hoped-for outcome of his endeavors. His vision took him somewhere distant.

I was freshly reminded of this visionary intention of Charlie's when Clara told me several days ago that when the carillon in Wait Chapel was being installed and the carillon bells were being inscribed, President Scales asked Charlie to provide an inscription for one of the bells. Charlie selected a quotation from the great Danish astronomer Tycho Brahe which he had previously used as a motto for a symposium on the fine arts held in preparation for the construction of the Scales Center. The quotation was as follows: "That this work of ours may lead to victories for the age to come. The victors may not remember us, and if so, what matter? For them shall be the joy, the victories and the praise. Ours will be the glory of the fathers in the sons."

Charlie wanted those sentences by Brahe read at this memorial service. Listen: "That this work of ours may lead to victories for the age to come."

Charlie also asked that other lines – from another writer – be read at the end of this service. The writer is Shakespeare, and the play is *The Tempest*, and the speaker is Prospero, who, in ways not totally unlike Charlie, was a magician who could summon up spirits from the air. Prospero speaks to Ferdinand:

You do look, my son, in a mov'd sort,
As if you were dismay'd. Be cheerful sir
Our revels now are ended. These our actors,
As I foretold you, were all spirits and
Are melted into air, into thin air;
And, like the baseless fabric of this vision,
The cloud-capp'd towers, the gorgeous palaces,
The solemn temples, the great globe itself,
Yea, all which it inherit, shall dissolve,
And, like this insubstantial pageant faded,
Leave not a rack behind. We are such stuff
As dreams are made on, and our little life
Is rounded with a sleep.

September 3, 2005

Willis Everette "Doc" Murphrey

Alumnus, Most Famous Cheerleader
Received the Medallion of Merit in 2005

My conservative Baptist father didn't really approve of motion pictures, but whenever a Will Rogers movie came to town, he went to the theatre. Once I asked him why he liked Will Rogers, and he said, "Because he's funny and he makes me feel good."

"Doc" Murphrey made people feel good wherever he went – whether in a circle of close friends gathered around him and listening, or at a Wake Forest alumni meeting where Deacons were telling stories, or in a football stadium where even apathetic spectators would jump up and pay attention whenever "Doc" stepped up onto the cheerleaders' platform. His very presence – his smile, his gestures, his straw hat – was enough to make people notice and watch and laugh and cheer, even at a game that we were losing.

Do you know what a rare quality that is? We rightly treasure professional achievement and success, and we value the intellect, and we honor those who are truly good, and "Doc" had all those virtues too. I would not for a moment overlook his fine career. He was an accomplished attorney, a community leader, a servant in good causes, and a devoted family man. But we Wake Foresters will remember "Doc" first, I think, because of his blessed sense of humor and the way he had of communicating that sense of humor to everyone around him.

You know, many people – lawyers, preachers, teachers, and the like – can make speeches, and many people can make us think. But how many people do you know who can tell us stories and make us laugh? I can think of only a few. And how much, in our confusing and chaotic and sometimes dangerous world, do we need laughter – not the cruel and degrading laughter that we so often hear on television, but laughter that is produced by someone who genuinely loves people and has a good heart and wants to make others happy? Laughter, after all, means sympathy. Will Rogers once said, "If a fellow doesn't have a good time once in a while and get a good laugh out of the serious side of life, he doesn't half live."

Perhaps because I love Wake Forest so much, I like to think that at least part of Doc Murphrey's personality came from the old campus – "little old Wake Forest" – where he and I – and many of us here today – went to school. I don't think I am exaggerating too much to say that we Wake Foresters respected each other and we appreciated each other and we loved each other. Our bonds of friendship are still with us – so much so that whenever I see Wake Forest people gathered together, as I do today, I know that I am at home.

And "Doc" Murphrey was at home too – wherever Old Gold and Black was "waving high." My favorite story of Doc's was one he often told about the time he was down town in old Wake Forest and he realized that, if he didn't hurry, he would be late for Dr. A.C. Reid's philosophy class. (As some of you know, Dr. Reid locked the classroom door when the bell rang.) "Doc" moved quickly so as to get to class, but a train was on the track just below those stairs that took you to the campus, and he couldn't get across the tracks. So he climbed into one of the boxcars. But then, unfortunately, the train started, and he couldn't get off. He went all the way to Henderson, he said.

My image of "Doc" Murphrey this afternoon is of seeing him on that Wake Forest train, standing at the boxcar door, smiling, taking off his hat, and saying "Goodbye."

And we look up at "Doc" and we say, "Goodbye 'Doc'. And thanks for a good life."

December 9, 2005

Thomas F. Gossett

English Faculty

To begin my remarks about Tom Gossett by saying that he was a scholar and a gentleman is to do no more than set the stage for remembering him. For Tom Gossett cannot easily be defined. One thing that is clear about him is that he is charmingly unforgettable. In recent days friends around the Wake Forest campus have laughed and cried over him, unwilling to believe that he will not again be walking – one more time – into the library in search of yet another errant piece of information or just looking for someone to tell a story to. You know, Tom was a sort of hovering presence: poking around and sorting out and happily doing research, sometimes expressing harsh opinions, especially when he was thinking about a sharp letter he wanted to write to the newspaper. But he had a twinkle in his eyes, and even when he became a little stern and let you know that he thought you were wrong about something, he could suddenly smile and enclose you in an aura of warmth and conviviality.

As a scholar Tom Gossett was widely recognized as the author of one of the best books on race in America. He did not wince from taking on this most difficult subject of his native South, and he explored historic, brutal racism with exacting research and ethical human understanding. He was scholar, ethicist, and observer, and he brought to his work another side of his complex nature: the patience and the solitude and the confidence of a man alone with his own thoughts.

In his private life Tom was also a mediator between people with opposing points of view. He truly hoped that old wounds – between individuals as well as races – could be healed and that disagreements could be laid to rest. Perhaps few of us knew that side of Tom – unless we were among those whom he sought to connect to each other. He was acquainted with folks of every kind: audiences at the Shepherd's Center where he taught, prisoners whom he counseled and wrote letters to, and also celebrated authors. Years ago in Georgia he was a friend of Flannery O'Connor, and here in Winston-Salem, he was the constant companion of the poet Archie Ammons when Archie was a visiting writer at Wake Forest and with his family lived across the street from Tom and Louise. We have in our library hours of tapes that Tom and Louise made of Archie reading his poetry and, as Tom loved to point out, with the voice of Napper Tandy, one of the Gossetts' favorite cats, in the background. ("I met with Napper Tandy, and he took me by the hand," the old song goes.) He and Louise made frequent visits to see retired members of the Wake Forest family. How many hours must Tom and Louise have spent "visiting": a word that has special meaning to those of us who are older – and Southern.

Do you experience a kind of envy when I tell you that Tom never had a television set? Why did he want one? There were too many other, better things to do than watch television. Music, for example. Concerts at Wake Forest, at Reynolda House, at the School of the Arts, at Salem, and all over town. Tom was a pianist himself, and he sometimes played at places like Independence Village. He was even known to play the piano and read a book at the same time. (He liked to play Scott Joplin, by the way.) Art? The walls of his house are filled with paintings, some of them by local artists who were his friends. And, of course, books! How often did he bring me a list of books he thought the library should have! Sometimes I thought he wanted the Z. Smith Reynolds Library to be like the Library of Congress and own every book ever published. And travel? Tom often recalled his months in London, especially during the term he led a group of students at Worrell House. ("Earth has not anything to show more fair.") And nature – the outdoors! He was an indefatigable bird watcher; he and Louise climbed Mt. LeConte eleven times; he spent happy hours in the summertime on a West Virginia farm; and the Gossetts' home was an almost holy shrine for cats – until Tom discovered that he was allergic to them.

At this time of year friends and neighbors awaited Tom's appointed rounds to deliver Louise's Christmas cookies, and though he insisted that he could not come in, if you persisted in your invitation, he'd stay just a few minutes. And, taking off his handsome coat and cap, he'd sit down and immediately want to tell you about a book he thought you'd want to read. Then, slapping his cap against his leg, he'd just as suddenly stand up and say, "I really must be going, Louise gave me instructions," then he'd be off.

Those of you who were Tom's friends know that the central fact of his life – the heart of his many busy and rewarding years – was Louise. Theirs was one of the enduring love stories I have known: a "marriage of true minds" to which there were no impediments. Together, they faced life with wisdom and with passion and with faith, hope, and love.

One of Tom's brothers who was in town this week recalls one day when he and another brother were waiting in a Texas airport for Tom to come in. Someone came to the terminal and announced that one of the passengers had left a suit on the plane. The brothers said, "Now we know that Tom has landed."

After a long and crowded and honorable life, we know today that Tom has "landed." I can imagine him now: slapping his cap against his leg and saying, "I really must be going."

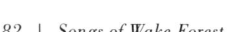

December 15, 2005

Egbert L. Davis, Jr.

Alumnus, Board of Trustees
Received the Medallion of Merit in 1976

Egbert Davis was a pioneer: one of the last survivors of what Shakespeare – speaking, of course, of his countrymen – called a "happy breed of men": men who in the twentieth century built this "little world" of ours that we call Winston-Salem. Like his father, like his brother Tom (a pathfinder in the sky), Egbert was a man of achievement and influence – in business, in education, in health care, in philanthropy, in the arts – and I could dwell at length on what he contributed in time, in energy, in wisdom, and in gifts to this community and, in particular, to Wake Forest University and to the School of Medicine and the Baptist Hospital. But I prefer, this afternoon, to remember him, somewhat more simply, as a person who, through all the years of his life and in the midst of many honors, never really changed in spirit or in outlook. He remained young, optimistic – still, somehow, almost a boy: in love with life and with people. What was so rare about his ninety-five years was that he never lost the capacity to be, in C.S. Lewis' words, "surprised by joy."

My own memories of Egbert go back to 1956, when, coming to Winston-Salem fifty years ago, as we of Wake Forest did, we were fortunate to be greeted by his welcoming hand and welcoming smile – and welcoming heart. Winston-Salem was his home, and he wanted it to be our home too.

We already knew the name of Egbert Davis, Egbert Jr.'s father. It was on the facade of one of the four men's dormitories that surrounded and graced the Quad: the only one of the four not named for a former Wake Forest president: surely, we realized, a singular tribute to a generous family. And Egbert Sr. lived on Reynolda Road, a short walk away from the campus.

Egbert Jr. lived a little further away on Arbor Road, and his stately home was to become familiar to many Wake Forest people. In 1956 I was a young English teacher, just a few years out of graduate school, and Egbert knew me only as a Wake Forest alumnus who had later been a member of his fraternity, and yet he asked me to come and have lunch with him and Eleanor: my very first invitation to a Winston-Salem home. I still remember the summer light coming into the sun porch where we sat and ate and talked. It was on that same sun porch, fifty years later, that – just a few weeks ago – I saw Egbert for the last time. He was still smiling.

So I hope it is all right with Egbert's family if I speak of him primarily as a friend rather than as a Trustee or a prominent citizen. I recall vividly being with him in Venice when we discovered what was to become the Wake Forest house, and, in President Scales's words, Egbert worked as "carpenter, plumber, and painter" while Eleanor and I went shopping for a tablecloth I could bring home as a present to my wife. (I knew that with Eleanor's help I would buy just the right thing.) And I remember how happy he was when we were in London and he went to the War Room

Davis speaks at the dedication of Casa Artom.

and sat, commandingly, in the very chair that Winston Churchill sat in during World War II cabinet sessions. And I remember him, no less enthusiastically, enjoying a simple meal on the train from Budapest to Vienna.

Of course, Egbert was a highly successful man of business, and he could be firm when the occasion required. I often watched him as he presided as chairman over the Wake Forest Board of Trustees. He would listen patiently to every opinion expressed, disagree politely if he was so inclined, and then move the group toward the decision he wanted. I recall with gratitude one occasion when one Trustee said that Wake Forest should abolish the foreign language requirement for entrance to the College; Egbert made it unmistakably clear that such a change would not take place on his watch: pretty sophisticated, I would say, for a boy from Yadkin County. He coveted the traditions embedded in the liberal arts, and he was a man of continuing and unshakable principle – in this respect and in so many others.

But most of all I see Egbert Davis as miraculously a happy man: whether playing with his electric trains, or coming hopefully – he was always hopeful – to the Coliseum for yet another basketball game (I remember the last time I saw him at a game, walking slowly, to be sure, but determinedly, down the steps to his seat), or – best of all – posing for one more Christmas card picture with his large and handsome and adoring family: all the generations together in one familiar place.

Davis and fellow trustees at Commencement

Today, I would say to all of us who knew Egbert Davis – and especially to the family he loved so much – that we should never forget to remember him. The world we live in is hurried and crowded and strangely distracted – and worried about the future – and we need, more than ever, to love life as it passes day by day, and we need to find peace and joy in the eternal moment. The prophet Isaiah said, "Look to the rock from which you were hewn, And to the quarry from which you were dug." We – Winston-Salem, Wake Forest, the Davis family – we are hewn from good rock and dug from a good quarry. Let us look to that rock and that quarry. Let us remain true to the enchanted ground on which we stand.

November 12, 2006

Paul Robinson

Music Faculty

NOT SO MANY MONTHS AGO, I saw Paul Robinson – at a concert, of course – and he was, as he always had been, alert, responsive, smiling, gentle, a touch of quiet amusement about where he was and what was going on. And I remembered the first time I saw him: in the fall of 1952, at a reception for new faculty members in President Tribble's front yard on the old campus. How much of our Wake Forest world has changed since 1952, I thought: a completely new campus, four different administrations, hundreds – thousands? – of teachers and students coming and going, the very landscape of the mind and heart. And yet here was Paul Robinson: retired for almost three decades, nearing his one hundredth birthday, still affirming what, after his wife and family, he loved most: great music.

In these more affluent, more comfortable times, in our days of increasing "success," I think we need to be reminded occasionally about where we came from and those men and women who preceded us to where we are. Before there was a music wing to the Scales Fine Arts Center, before there was a Brendle Hall, before the necessary resources arrived to create a music department such as we have today, four faculty members – Thane McDonald, Chris Giles, Lucille Harris, and Paul Robinson – with the help now and then of part-time adjunct teachers – kept music alive on the old campus, transferred that commitment to Winston-Salem, and – in crowded quarters, with a severely limited budget – built the foundation for what we now, in our fine music department, admire and enjoy.

Paul Robinson was at the heart of Wake Forest music for twenty-seven years. He was, of course, best known and most visible as our University organist: playing here in Wait Chapel, on I don't know how many occasions, when a prelude or a postlude or something in between was called for; performing – for 37 years! – at Sunday morning services in the Wake Forest Baptist Church; serving as accompanist for the community's traditional December production of Handel's *The Messiah*. Always available, always ready and disciplined, always sensitive to the nuances of sound and stress, always – because of his innate modesty – almost invisible, Paul brought to everything he played understanding and dignity and unerring taste.

I like to recall that Paul had his own private pipe organ in the house on Faculty Drive that he and Mary Frances built: a house, Mary Frances says, that was designed more to make a space for the organ than to take care of the other needs of the family. (That organ, by the way, is now at Knollwood Baptist Church.) And I am pleased by two recollections in particular: the time that Paul, having agreed to present to the fondly lamented faculty Humanities Club a history of the group, read a sly and impish account of the years of the Club's existence; and an utterly different evening in Paris, when my daughter Sally and I, both of us wide-eyed travelers, went with Paul and Mary Frances to a charming and chic restaurant on Paris' Left Bank. As some of you old-timers know, that was quite a stretch: from the staid Wake Forest Humanities Club to the lively Latin Quarter. Paul made the transition without effort.

In Robert Browning's poem, "Abt Vogler" the organist takes his place at the keyboard, bids the organ obey, calls the keys to their work, and builds his "manifold music." As he does so, he comes to a realization of his unique strength as an organist. Others "may reason and welcome," he says, "tis we musicians [who] know." And he continues:

Give me the keys. I feel for the common chord again, Sliding by semitones, till I sink to the minor, – yes, And I blunt it into a ninth, and I stand on alien ground, Surveying awhile the heights I rolled from into the deep;

Which, hark, I have dared and done, for my resting-place is found. [I have found] The C Major of ... life; so, now I will try to sleep.

From left: Music Professors Huber, Halpern, Harris, Robinson, Kalter and McDonald

Today I imagine Paul Robinson at a familiar keyboard: active but unobtrusive, confident and content, once more "surveying the heights" of music. And I think to myself, "Blessed are the pure in heart." Paul was "pure in heart." And, because of that, he blessed us too.

March 4, 2007

Bill Angell
Alumnus, Religion Faculty

The year is 1940. The place is the college town of Wake Forest. The setting is the once-upon-a-time Alumni Building. The room is a large, light, and airy space on the third floor where English professors prepare their classes and where student assistants grade freshman themes – at the standard rate of thirty cents an hour.

It was in that room on one long-ago afternoon that I met Bill Angell. He was a senior; I was a sophomore. We were both grading papers. I knew at once that he was a talented and generous person. A devout and confirmed Baptist, he was ecumenically hospitable – those words were to have an important resonance in his career – to those like me who were outside the Baptist fold. A student of theology, he read perceptively and avidly the secular novels and plays in Broadus Jones's and Edgar Folk's courses in contemporary literature. A deep-rooted Southerner, he welcomed Franklin Roosevelt's New Deal and wore the dreaded "L" word with pride and approval. He was – in short – a believing Baptist, a man of broad learning and culture, and a political and social liberal: a microcosmic representative of what I for one have always thought was Wake Forest at its best.

Bill graduated the following spring. I did not, of course, know whether I would see him again except perhaps at some future Homecoming. Neither of us could have predicted – although we might have hoped for it that circumstances would bring us back to the College we loved and that we would become life-long friends. But fifteen years after we met, we were back here to stay.

Bill's years away from Wake Forest – in extended studies in America and in Europe – brought him many valuable experiences and new learning and maturity. They also, fortunately, brought Marjorie: her musical gifts, her refined tastes for hearth and home, her poise and grace. Bill and Marjorie settled in a charmingly original contemporary house on Belle Vista Court where it became the good fortune of many of us to enjoy the comforts of their living room, with sounds of keyboard and strings, and the gourmet delights of Marjorie's dining room and kitchen.

For thirty-five years as a Wake Forest religion professor Bill Angell taught, wrote – many books and articles – preached, advised, was a compassionate neighbor, served honorably in all things. He adapted with wisdom to the changing needs and customs of generations of students. He ventured happily into new arenas: the innovative and ground-breaking course in "Meaning and Value in Western Thought" that he shared with his old friend Bobby Helm; the Ecumenical Institute (Baptists and Catholics working together) that he and Carlton Mitchell kept alive and vibrant; the joys of being a father and then a grandfather. In debates and crises he kept a sense of humor which was self-deprecating and kind and was always, somehow, a visible sign of how well he understood himself and the purpose of his life. And in all important ways he remained the same Bill Angell I had met more than half a century ago: a believing Baptist, a man of broad learning and culture, and a liberal. (I invite you to read a fascinating paper he wrote ten years ago for a local audience. It is called "In Praise of Liberalism: Exorcizing a Demon." He compared conservatism and liberalism to an automobile. Conservatism is the brakes. Liberalism is the engine. But, he said, more important than either the motor or the brakes is the driver who operates both.)

The *Winston-Salem Journal*, several days ago, said that Bill was 87 years old. His family and friends know that, far from being 87, he was not quite 22. For, you see, he was born on February 29 – in a Leap Year – and so he had had fewer birthdays than most of us. Maybe that was why he remained so young at heart. In the book on "Meaning and Value" that he and Bob Helm wrote, they said, echoing Jesus, that "true happiness" is "in being rather than in having." "To be" rather than "to have": that suggests the inner spirit that Bill, again and again, radiated all through his 87 – or, rather, his almost 22 – years.

The poet Wordsworth once wrote about a truly "happy" man. It is he, Wordsworth said,

who, when brought
Among the tasks of real life, hath wrought
Upon the plan that pleased his boyish thought
Whose high endeavours are an inward light
That makes the path before him always bright
Who, with a natural instinct to discern
What knowledge can perform, is diligent to learn;
Abides by this resolve, and stops not there,
But makes his moral being his prime care.

Bill Angell made "his moral being his prime care," and he gave to Wake Forest and to all his friendships an open mind, a committed conscience, an amused awareness of the ironies of the human condition, greetings of kindness and concern, a long and tolerant and hopeful view of life, a deep and abiding faith, and, when Marjorie was nearby, all was accompanied by the strains of joyful music. Let us remember him with gratitude and love.

September 14, 2007

Julian Burroughs
Alumnus, Radio/Film/TV Faculty

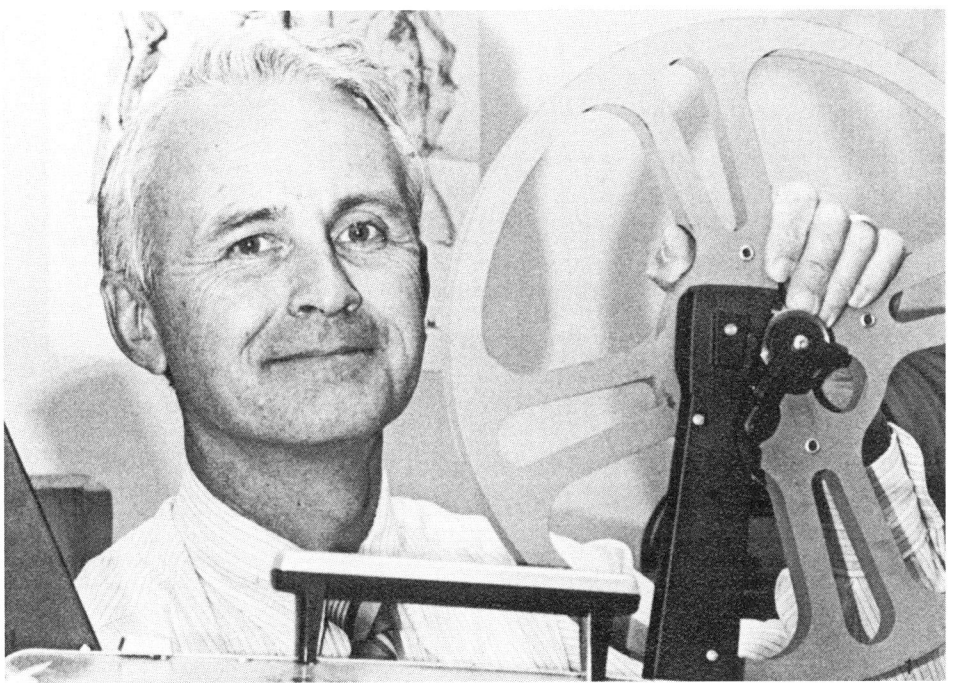

NOT LONG AGO, Julian Burroughs told the story of his long and rich life. Here is part of what he remembered.

A native of Rockingham, North Carolina, Julian was born March 19, 1928, to Julian and Ruby Morton Burroughs. His mother was the founding director of the Rockingham Merchants Association, and his father was a long-time drug store operator in Red Springs. Julian's stepfather, Don Sedberry, was the owner of Sedberry Funeral Home in Rockingham and Anson Memorial Park in Wadesboro.

He enjoyed growing up in a small town and cherished the many childhood friends be developed in the Rockingham School System. He loved his teachers – they nurtured his interests in debate, public speaking, drama and sports. He was voted Best-All-Round his senior year and was captain of the football team and leading actor in the Dramatic Club. He represented Rockingham in the American Legion Oratorical contest. He was the president of his senior class.

Upon graduation from Rockingham High, Julian enlisted in the U.S. Army and served 13 months in the U.S. Army of Occupation in Korea. He was honorably discharged at the rank of Staff Sergeant.

He returned home in 1948 and entered Wake Forest College, where he majored in English and participated in theatre before joining the campus radio station, WFDD, as an announcer. He served as Student Station Manager his senior year.

After completing his degree at Wake Forest, Julian taught for a year at Riverside Military Academy in Gainesville, Georgia, followed by a three-year teaching position at Williams High School in Burlington.

There he taught American History, Speech and Drama, coached the debate team, and produced state champion drama winners.

It was while teaching in Burlington that Julian met his wife of 53 years, Jean Miller, his "diva" whose singing in Burlington, at Meredith College and at the University of Michigan, brought her wide recognition and advanced degrees.

Both Julian and Jean left Burlington in 1955 to pursue graduate studies at the University of Michigan. They came to Winston-Salem in 1958, when Julian was offered a position at Wake Forest. A year later, Jean began her 35-year career as vocal and choral instructor and director of the fine arts program at Salem Academy.

In addition to his 36-year faculty tenure at Wake Forest, Julian founded the public radio station, WFDD-FM, and served as its director for 23 years. He was among the station representatives who helped to create National Public Radio in the late 1960s.

After attending the University of Southern California Film School in 1968, Julian introduced a series of film courses that became the foundation of the Film Studies Program at Wake Forest.

Julian traveled with the debate team and produced plays for the Wake Forest University theatre. He directed numerous speech, drama and film workshops and Readers Theatre productions. He acted with the Winston-Salem Little Theatre and Tanglewood Barn Theatre.

While directing WFDD, Julian produced hundreds of educational radio programs for the Winston-Salem Community Radio-TV Council, and over the years he produced numerous educational films and videos, as well as educational radio programs for the National Association of Educational Broadcasters. He also wrote articles and reviews for various professional journals.

For over 40 years Julian and Jean were devoted members of the Wake Forest Baptist Church. They still count among their dearest friends members of that church. In 1998 they became members here at Centenary United Methodist Church, where they have found a loving, caring group of Christians who have renewed and sustained them in that fellowship. Both have served on major church councils and committees, devoting themselves

especially to the Senior Adult Council and the Faith and Arts Committee.

When Julian retired to become Professor Emeritus of Communication in 1994, he took up a retirement career as a painter and sculptor and found much joy in his association with art teachers and students throughout the community. He has had several solo exhibitions of his works and has participated in numerous group showings. He also began to play his clarinet again and had many happy music experiences with the New Horizons Band directed by Peter Perret, and he delighted in his clarinet lessons with Linda Julian, his teacher.

Jean also retired in 1994 from her position at Salem Academy, and together they took on a new life that included grandparenting, regular rounds of golf – always WALKING together – and yearly travel to Europe and the western USA.

Julian has also been blessed by two daughters (Catherine and Lee), two devoted and caring sons-in-law (Scott and Rick), two half-sisters, and three grandsons (Parker, Brooks, and Nicholas). Parker now lives in the freshman dormitory 100 yards across from the Burroughses' Faculty Drive home. Both daughters graduated from Salem

Academy and from Wake Forest University. Both are teachers.

The last time Julian felt like getting out and about was on December 29 when the family celebrated Wake Forest's bowl victory in Charlotte. A year earlier, all the family had enjoyed the Orange Bowl trip to Miami. For it was and is Wake Forest that makes up the larger Burroughs family. So go the Deacons and so go the Burroughses.

What an appropriate last sentence for Julian's own story of his life! "So go the Deacons and so go the Burroughses!"

Now, I would like to add a few thoughts of my own to what Julian himself has told us and to speak of certain essential qualities of the man that facts alone cannot fully reveal. I speak as a long-time friend and colleague.

Obviously, Julian's pioneering achievements with WFDD will always be central in his life story: a studio at the station has already been named in his honor. And his special role in introducing film studies to the college curriculum will continue to be appreciated. But I want to recall a more underlying theme to his life: the persuasive and gentle ways in which he practiced and kept alive the best ideals and traditions of Wake Forest. Words like "integrity" and "virtue" and "faith" do not perhaps come as easily to mind as they once did, but these words are woven into the fabric of Wake Forest, and they are part of Wake Forest's historic mission. Julian embraced that mission and wove his own creative design into that fabric. He not only loved Wake Forest; he honored it. To give that kind of honor to a cause, to a family, to a life is the true test of a man; Julian passed that test with affection and strength, and it is primarily as a man of character and steadfastness that his memory will be cherished by his family and friends and by the University that he loved.

May 12, 2008

Elizabeth Phillips

English Faculty
Received the Medallion of Merit in 1992

ONCE, WHEN I WAS GOING TO introduce Elizabeth Phillips for a speech, I asked her whether there was anything she would like for me to say about her. "I'd like for you to tell them," she said, "That I come from Spruce Pine, North Carolina." That was her only suggestion. Was she joking, I thought, or was being from Spruce Pine a mysterious clue to her identity – like Rosebud for Citizen Kane or, more appropriately, Kirkwood, Missouri, for Marianne Moore?

When I first met Elizabeth, she didn't *seem* like a native of Spruce Pine. The year was 1957. Wake Forest, only twelve months in Winston-Salem, was still a strict and thoroughly traditional college; and faculty members, for the most part, were pleasantly and happily conformist to customs brought from the old campus. Elizabeth was hardly typical. She was straightforward. She was skeptical. She was shrewdly informed about rebellious strains in contemporary literature. She was audacious when the occasion required. She was – before the word came into wide popular usage – "liberated." A liberated woman on the 1957 Wake Forest campus: in ways we could not have then foreseen, she predicted, and she prepared us for, our future.

We now realize, half a century later, that Elizabeth Phillips was, for all her years, a "liberator." Younger women, as some of you know better than I, looked to her as a pioneer and as an exemplar: someone who challenged conventions, who stood firm, who made today possible. Without her tenacity and toughness – mingled, I should say, with wise diplomacy –

some of you would not be here this afternoon. Blacks also knew her as their friend: Maya Angelou has already confirmed the unique place Elizabeth had in her heart.

May I say that men, too, owed a debt to Elizabeth: she encouraged us in our sensitivity, in our emotional candor, in what is best about our maleness: and she always illuminated the human values that make all of us – men and women, young and old – at once so worthy and so vulnerable.

For Elizabeth did not believe in any kind of aristocracy. She was a true democrat, a true egalitarian. No human being lay outside her esteem.

And where did this democratic spirit, this love for people – both so old-fashioned and so modern – come from? Might it have come from Spruce Pine? Could that be the meaning to the clue she gave me?

Those of you who have not come to know North Carolina well may not realize how many men and women there are in this state who believe passionately in equality and in freedom. You also may not know how many of these men and women have been nurtured in our western mountains, where they have learned to be strong, to be independent, to speak their thoughts, and to fear no one.

Elizabeth Phillips was such a North Carolina mountain woman.

Her roots were deep in the soil from which so much strength comes. And that heritage both freed her, and imposed upon her a powerful sense of responsibility and obligation. For Elizabeth understood liberation as leading not to frivolity but rather to duty. And from that understanding, I think, came what was so refreshing and so admirable about her and about her years at Wake Forest.

How many times, early in the morning or late at night, did I see her light burning at home and catch a glimpse of her reading or grading papers or working on a manuscript! How often did returning students seek her out for counsel or for friendship and find themselves treated to coffee or a drink or a meal! How remarkable it is that her three books on American poets were all published in the last crowded decade of her active years as a teacher!

Elizabeth, this free and spontaneous woman, was one of the most thoroughly responsible people I ever knew. She taught her classes, she wrote her books, she welcomed students with time and courtesy – and yet she was always available for additional tasks. I never knew her to refuse appointment to a committee because she was too busy, and I never knew her, when serving on a committee, to be other than active and informed. And she took upon herself – as so few of her colleagues did – the obligation of being where she thought she ought to be: at a faculty meeting, at a reading by a visiting poet, at a lecture by an alumnus she once knew, at a Martin Luther King celebration or a gospel choir performance, at a University convocation, at a memorial service: wherever there was a need to declare, to support, to commend, to appreciate, to comfort, to remember.

From left: Elizabeth Phillips with colleagues Edward Lobb and Dolly McPherson

For Elizabeth was, most of all, a kind and generous person: generous to listen, generous to entertain, generous to cherish, and generous to love.

September 3, 2008

Henry Stroupe

*Alumnus, History Faculty,
Dean of Graduate School,
Received the Medallion of Merit in 1998*

Every now and then – especially during these more affluent and more expansive times – it is instructive and, I think, therapeutic to look back with gratitude to those strong-shouldered men and women whose wholehearted devotion to Wake Forest created the foundation for what we see all around us today. With limited facilities, with few dollars, sometimes with little support beyond what their own energy supplied, they answered a call to service and remained ever faithful to that call – "constant and true," as we say in the words of our "Alma Mater."

This memorial service today gives us such an occasion to look back, for Henry Stroupe was one of those "strong-shouldered" men: not alone because he stood tall and erect – his posture and presence still reminding us that he had been a naval officer in World War II – but because he was clear in his head about the principles that mattered to him, and he followed those principles – always efficiently; sometimes, perhaps, even tenaciously; but for reasons that had nothing to do with self-glorification. His "old campus" neighbor, Professor D. A. Brown, once said to me that, when he looked out in the morning and saw Henry coming by on his way to work, he knew what time it was. Henry, he said, was as dependable as a clock.

I first encountered Henry Stroupe when I was a sophomore and enrolled in his two-semester course in American history. We met in the large lecture room of the old Social Science Building which had, it seems hard to believe, once served as the College gymnasium. His lectures were clear and precise and allowed little room for irony or ambiguity. With a manner that was direct and straightforward, he guided us down the American path from Plymouth Rock and Jamestown all the way to the New Deal and the beginnings of the Second World War. I am still thankful for having been given a framework and a background that continue to enrich my understanding of the course of U.S. history.

In that crucial summer of 1956, when so many things about Wake Forest changed, Henry and most of his faculty colleagues brought to the Winston-Salem campus those things about Wake Forest which they did not want to change: the importance of teaching, a close community of faculty and students, a nearby neighborhood of faculty homes, the virtues of friendliness and honor, a belief that the story of Wake Forest, in spite of bleak and disappointing moments in its history, had been, in essence, noble and heroic. Henry Stroupe was here in Winston-Salem to stay, and he was ready and eager to teach in a new setting.

But he did much more than teach. He became chairman of the history department and presided over the recruitment of some of Wake Forest's most imaginative and most popular history teachers. The 1960's were a lively and flourishing decade for the discipline of history and for the increasing versatility of those who taught it.

In 1967, when the College became a University and, in response to an oft-expressed conviction by President Harold Tribble that graduate programs should be developed, Henry, who had already been director of graduate studies, became the first Dean of the Graduate School. During his seventeen years in that office he oversaw the creation of a number of M.A. programs, and three Ph.D.s: in biology, in chemistry and in physics. Much of what is best about our Graduate School today is the result of his patient and dedicated leadership.

It has been twenty-five years since Henry retired, but he never wavered in his love for Wake Forest or in his love for life. With Elizabeth, his beloved wife of sixty-seven years, at his side, he continued to stand tall. I am perhaps the least qualified person available to speak about his enthusiasm for golf or the admirable way in which he kept his immaculate lawn, since I am neither a golfer nor a gardener, but I can – and I do – admire success in any endeavor, and I know that in whatever Henry attempted, he found pleasure and strength.

When I think of Henry this afternoon, one image from an old and much-loved hymn comes unbidden to my mind: Henry Stroupe was "like a tree planted by the water." May we remember him gratefully.

August 25, 2009

McLeod Bryan

Alumnus, Religion Faculty

I WOULD FIRST LIKE TO SAY that my wife Emily, a devoted friend and admirer of Mac Bryan, joins me this afternoon in this tribute and in expressing our sympathy and love for Mac's family.

Mac Bryan and I were students on the old campus of Wake Forest College. The College was thought by some, I suppose, to have been a somewhat placid, sheltered, comfortable place, insulated from the troubles of the world, but there was an occasional student who looked beyond the borders of the campus and saw poverty and discrimination and racial injustice and decided to go out after graduation to speak and to fight against what he thought was wrong. One such young man was Bill Finlator; another was Will Campbell – both of them friends of Mac Bryan. And then there was Mac himself.

I can't say what might have impelled Mac – out of his own reading of the Gospels, from Wake Forest classes that he took, from experiences in the places where he lived and worked between his graduation in 1940 and his return to the new Wake Forest campus as a religion professor in 1956 – what impelled him, that is, to become, almost from the first, Wake Forest's acknowledged spokesman for the liberal causes of his lifetime. There were doubtless many of his colleagues who agreed with his principles and his goals, and I think that the institution itself, founded as a place "Pro Humanitate," knew, deeply inside its better self, that Mac was right.

But most of us held back. Lest I seem to be critical only of others, let me admit that I – for one – was cautious, careful, privately admiring Mac Bryan and supporting him behind the scenes, but not joining him on some platform or in some assembly where, as was often the case, he stood alone.

An authority on African Culture, Professor Bryan looks over artifacts which he collected in Tanzania.

But Mac did not wait for approval from either faculty or administration. Wherever there was a cause he believed in, his voice could be heard: during every stage of the civil rights movement, in opposition to the war in Vietnam, in support of the impeachment of Richard Nixon, in defense of a young professor who had been denied tenure, against every manifestation of intolerance or injustice or unfairness. And I remember – still with some surprise – the outdoor picnics he and Edna had at their home in the 1960s in honor of new African heads of state who had led their countries to liberty from European colonialism. Mac always rejoiced in witnessing and supporting any such freedom from oppression.

I like using the word "rejoice" because it reminds me that Mac was almost always joyful. He could be somber, of course, but a smile, if not always there, was lurking to be noticed. And I hope that in recent years he could look at his alma mater and at his friends and colleagues and know that, on the central issues of social justice, he was right. And I hope also that he realized in his later years that Wake Forest – the institution that he and I (and many others here this afternoon) loved and served – is a far better place – more open, more diverse, more inclusive, more willing to embrace the world – because he brought to his lifelong and prophetic mission, knowledge, commitment, courage, hope, and joy. His legacy has surely become a permanent part of the history and the legacy of Wake Forest.

October 3, 2010

Robert Beck

Psychology Faculty

THE STORY OF PSYCHOLOGY at Wake Forest is, in large part, the story of Bob Beck. He came here in 1959 when Wake Forest was still, officially, a College and when Psychology was in the process of being created as a department, and, until he retired fifty years later, he was a dependably constant and stabilizing force in the Department. During his long tenure, psychology became one of Wake Forest's most flourishing, most popular, and most productive departments, and Bob brought to the Department not just his talents in teaching and scholarship, but – even more important perhaps – his integrity, his innate sense of fairness, his good humor in difficult times. Not many faculty members have ever served, as he did, under four administrations, and what strikes me, as I reflect on his career, was how much, out of pleasure in his work and love for Wake Forest, he helped to shape that part of the Wake Forest of today that is most precious and most enduring, and that is destined to outlast the fashions of the moment.

I also like to think of Bob as he was in our faculty neighborhood, where he was always ready and eager to create opportunities for people to get together and have fun. I remember the block parties he arranged on July the Fourth, and in particular I see him happily encouraging children toward sports and games. There were sixteen children in our immediate neighborhood – eight boys and eight girls – and toward the boys especially Bob was coach and mentor. My son, one of the eight boys, has told me that of all the fathers in our families Bob was the one most active athletically and most generous with his time. He was blessed with an easy manner and an amiable disposition, and the boys truly liked him. If there had been an election, Bob would certainly have been named mayor.

Professor Beck monitoring equipment in his laboratory

Bob's interest in sports went beyond the neighborhood. Having come to the South at a time when soccer was not yet popular, he became an early spokesman in behalf of soccer: in high schools, at Wake Forest, or through a Youth Soccer Association that he helped found. On campus he chaired a committee to conduct one of the faculty's most successful studies into the relationship between academics and athletics. The "Beck Committee," as it became known, came forward with recommendations that are still foundational.

Our friend and neighbor Tom Mullen said to me recently that one of Bob's strongest and most appealing qualities was that he was clear headed and eminently reasonable and that he could be counted on to give a completely unbiased and unprejudiced opinion on any subject.

Bob's daughter Amy said a few days ago that Bob "was happy going to Wake Forest every day of his life." I can think of no more endearing comment, and I am grateful that Bob was with us for so many years to share that happiness with me and with all his many friends.

September 10, 2011

Allen Mandelbaum

Kenan Professor of the Humanities

These remarks were given at an informal gathering of friends.

WHEN I WAS A FIFTEEN-YEAR-OLD boy, reading Vergil's *Aeneid* carefully, awkwardly, translating the Latin lines, "I sing of arms and the man" and so on – I could not possibly have foreseen myself here tonight, standing near this honored man: a man who, at one of his early appearances here at Wake Forest, read some of those very lines I remembered from my high school Latin class, speaking out "loud and bold," as Keats would have said. In fact, like Keats, I was "like some watcher of the skies / When a new planet swims into his ken; / Or like stout Cortez when with eagle eyes / He stared at the Pacific."

For, you see, Allen Mandelbaum deserves to be *heard*. He should be read, of course. I need not list the books that carry his name; they are there, one after another, on your program, and they will endure beyond the life of his voice. But to *hear* Allen is to engage the man himself – it is of the *man* that I sing – and how fortunate we have been for the nineteen years he has been at Wake Forest. We have found out what others before us had already discovered: he is truly "large"; like Whitman, he "contains multitudes."

"Multitudes," indeed! I remember being with him at the Italian Cultural Institute in New York City when he was honored for his new verse translation of *The Metamorphoses* of Ovid,

a stunningly beautiful book in word and in design. I recall, happily, having lunch with him at an outdoor cafe in Bergamo, Italy; following his suggestion that I order the *osso buco*, I had one of the best meals I have ever had. Not long ago, I saw him at a production of *La Traviata*, raising his arms back and forth in tune with Verdi's great arias; I once talked with him

about Irish tenors singing Irish melodies, and he suggested I listen to Frank Patterson sing (I bought a Patterson CD); we once discussed basketball players, and I mentioned Winston-Salem's Earl Monroe, and he said, "Do you mean Earl the Pearl?" "Multitudes," indeed!

But these are mere footnotes to Allen's remarkable career and to the way in which he seems to encompass all learning. Here tonight at this celebration, in addition to the expected teachers of literature foreign and domestic, I see a virtual conclave of philosophers, a chemist, an economist, a lawyer, a doctor, and a cluster of librarians from the building that Allen so much likes to visit. (Do you librarians know how much Allen Mandelbaum honors and respects you? Almost every time I see him, he wants to thank you for all you do. Lesser faculty members may sometimes take you for granted, but our most distinguished scholar knows what you mean to him and to Wake Forest.) And, of course, I see Lily Saade, than whom no one among us is more perceptive and more faithful. She has much of the same cosmopolitanism that Allen had.

You will forgive someone of my age, I hope, when I say that Allen Mandelbaum represents a generation of scholars that we are not likely to see again. These days, we may talk hopefully about becoming more "international" or more "global" or more "interdisciplinary," but, in truth, I fear, we are much more likely to become increasingly provincial, retreating not only to our own various academic departments but even to corners of those departments. Who among us now, or who among those to come after us, will know and translate Latin, will know and translate Greek, will read Hebrew, will read and speak English and Italian with equal fluency, will be familiar with other European languages, will edit two volumes of American poetry, and meanwhile will write five books of his own poetry – at the same time teaching, advising students, and winning honors at home and abroad? And who will bring to his students Allen's deeply religious outlook that is so powerfully nurtured by Judaism but is also so passionately sympathetic toward Christianity?

William Butler Yeats, on a visit to Dublin's Municipal Gallery, looked at portraits, one after another, of the men and women of Ireland whom he most admired. "I am in despair," he said, "that time may bring / Approved patterns of women or of men / But not that selfsame excellence again." Tonight, in my imagination, I look at a gallery wall, and I see Germaine Bree, and I see Allen Mandelbaum, and I borrow Yeats's words: can time ever bring "that selfsame excellence again"? Who will be able to mount that "high horse" that Homer rode?

October 13, 2012

Mary Frances Robinson
Romance Languages Faculty

WHEN MARY FRANCES MC-FEETERS came to Wake Forest in 1952, she joined a faculty that she at once became an active and happy part of. A teacher of language and literature, she believed fervently in Wake Forest's liberal arts traditions. The daughter of overseas missionaries, she understood and treasured the College's historic denominational roots. As a near contemporary of hers, I can testify to how quickly she embraced Wake Forest and how quickly Wake Forest embraced her. And that embrace became more deeply personal and more endearing when three years later she married another newcomer, the musician/organist Paul Robinson, who by then had also become an integral part of a close-knit faculty.

During the memorable year of the College's great move to Winston-Salem, Mary Frances and Paul came along with their colleagues; they built a house on Faculty Drive, were blessed by the arrival of two daughters, and continued with steadfastness and energy to serve Wake Forest with their talents and their unfailing friendship.

But – to return for a moment to

Mary Frances' arrival in 1952 – she was then, in a way that we now recognize as historic, somewhat different from all but a few of the faculty members with whom she began to associate. She was – simply – a woman in a virtually all-male setting, the first female faculty member in Wake Forest history, in fact, to have earned a Ph.D.

And she later became – along with Elizabeth Phillips in English – the first woman to be a full professor and, subsequently, the first woman to be a department chairman: a position she held for several terms. Her place in the story of women at Wake Forest thus became significant and unique.

I recall especially the discussions that Mary Frances and I had in the early 1970's when she proposed that Romance Languages start a Semester in France program at the University in Dijon. At that time Casa Artom was our only overseas venture, having opened one year earlier, and very few students went abroad. Mary Frances took the first group of students to Dijon herself – in 1972 – and returned again and again, always with delight and imagination.

In spite of her pioneering achievements, Mary Frances did not call attention to herself – any more than did her unfailingly polite and considerate husband. She worked quietly and effectively to advance her department and the College and gave her talents to Wake Forest for thirty-seven years. I never knew her to be other than patiently dedicated to the highest ideals of her profession. She also continued to study and learn, occasionally auditing College courses outside her own discipline.

Mary Frances and Paul loved to travel – here and there around the world – to France, of course; to Egypt, where she grew up; and to whatever destination beckoned. I am happy to recall that, in 1989 – a year memorable to me because it was the 200th anniversary of the French Revolution – my college student daughter Sally and I were in Paris, and Mary Frances and Paul entertained us in a Left Bank restaurant where the setting was enchanting, the food incomparably delicious, and the company thoroughly Parisian. This afternoon I smile with gratitude as I see Sally and me and Mary Frances and Paul sharing a meal together. It sums up my personal fondness for Mary Frances – and, of course, for Paul.

Professor Robinson visits Auxerre Cathedral with a group of students in 1982 during their semester abroad in Dijon, France.

September 2, 2012

Tom Elmore
Alumnus, Dean's Office, Education Faculty

AT MY FIRST MEETING with Tom Elmore – it was in my office in the Alumni Building on the old Wake Forest campus – I knew that he had promise, and I suspected that he would fulfill that promise somewhere in the academic world. He was obviously gifted, but – more than that – he was eager to learn, on fire to get the most out of every day of college. If he heard about some subject that interested him, he wanted to investigate it and explore it as deeply as he could.

Tom graduated from Wake Forest in 1956, studied at Vanderbilt, received a Ph.D. from Ohio State, and returned to his alma mater in 1962. Except for six years in graduate schools, he thus lived his entire adult life at Wake Forest, and his love for Wake Forest was all-embracing. Even in retirement he was often on campus for some event that attracted his attention.

For eight years – from 1963 to 1971 – Tom was Dean of Students, working with Deans Mark Reece and Lu Leake during what were perhaps the most passionate and turbulent years in modern College history. Unlike many American colleges which experienced severe damage to campus order and decorum, Wake Forest remained essentially at peace and united. Much of that calmness was due to Tom Elmore, who – with dignity and persuasiveness – talked with students, individually and in groups, about their responsibilities and obligations to the community at large.

Tom left the central administration in 1971 in order to give himself full-time to teaching and to founding and directing Wake Forest's programs in counseling. It was in those programs, undergraduate and graduate, that Tom created a Wake Forest legacy that will always be associated with his name and bring him recognition and honor. No one can testify more faithfully to

that legacy than his student, friend, and ally Sam Gladding.

Tom's thirst for learning never left him. Even as recently as early this fall, I saw him at programs and lectures at Wake Forest. He truly had a "hungry heart." He did not want to miss any opportunity to educate himself further, usually in fields other than his own. I remember that, after he had traveled in Ireland, he wanted to learn more and more about Celtic myths and traditions. And that hunger for knowledge remained strong and never satisfied as long as he lived.

I don't know how many Wake Forest alumni were influenced by Tom's example and by his friendship. I like to think that, because of his example, they became more kind, more compassionate, and more willing to serve others. Those are certainly the qualities he had that I like most to remember. He was a true and faithful friend.

November 2, 2012

Carlton Mitchell

Alumnus, Religion Faculty

I KNEW CARLTON MITCHELL when he was an undergraduate and became quickly aware those long years ago that he was an accomplished and remarkably versatile young man. He was studying for the ministry: one of a number of such students who prospered intellectually in a Wake Forest atmosphere that encouraged far-seeing and progressive thought. He was also captain of the Murray Greason-coached basketball team and – perhaps known only to me among those who are here today – he took part in the College Theatre production of *Wuthering Heights*. The Theatre had been in existence for only a year – founded after Wake Forest's historic admission of women – and Carlton played the handsome and passionate Heathcliff. His co-star as Catherine Earnshaw was Wake Forest's first coed, the enchanting Beth Perry.

I know – certainly not from my own experience – but from the testimony of others – that basketball as his sport gave way to successfully competitive golf, and I am not aware of any later roles he might have had on the theatrical stage, but his preparation for the ministry led him to a chaplaincy in the Navy, to graduate studies, to church pulpits, and – in 1961 – to Wake Forest's Department of Religion. Bill Leonard will speak, I am sure, of Carlton as pastor, preacher, and teacher of religion.

I would like to remember him today, first of all, as a stalwart and dedicated member of the faculty who responded to every call for service. He was, for instance, chairman of his department at a time when department opinions were numerous and conflicting – is that always true of religion departments? I know it is true of English departments – and with a combination of kindness, fairness, and shrewd wisdom he steered the department (he was a Navy man, after all) safely and successfully. For three years he directed a Luce Foundation-sponsored lecture series on "Religion and the Social Crisis" and was series editor of the publications that followed. I also remember with pleasure that, characteristically of the centrality of his role as a faculty member, he was state president of the AAUP.

In – and beyond – the Department of Religion and academe, Carlton had an abiding love for all that was best about Wake Forest. He treasured every facet of Wake Forest's history, and he embraced the life around him in all its healthful manifestations. In practically every reunion of the Class of 1943 in recent years he was at the center – chairing committees, writing letters to classmates, showing a personal interest in every alumnus. (He was that kind of person.) And during the years when he chaired the Half-Century Club he showed the same openness to ideas, the same willingness to listen to everybody, the same unpretentious courtesy that was always part of his appealing personality.

From right: Carlton Mitchell with Allen Easley and Egbert Davis, Jr.

It is tempting on an occasion like this to list facts and achievements – and I have done that, of course – but ultimately what we remember about a friend is the inner self that caused us to admire and love him. What I saw most of all in Carlton was an unalloyed integrity, his – and this is an old-fashioned word – his virtue. In a poem called "Virtue" – a favorite poem, by the way, of Carlton's mentor, Allen Easley – the English poet George Herbert said, "Only a sweet and virtuous soul, / Like seasoned timber, never gives." Carlton Mitchell was "seasoned timber." He reached out to a full life, he reached out to people, and – like "seasoned timber" – he had a natural, inbred strength that marked him all his life.

February 16, 2013

Mary Anne Maynard
Alumnus, Wife of Dr. C. Douglas Maynard, Wake Forest School of Medicine

MAY I TAKE YOU BACK WITH me to another time, another place? The time is a September morning in 1955. The place is the lobby of the Alumni Building on the old Wake Forest campus. I have just entered the building, on my way to a freshman English class, and I see a most charming young woman, and we talk. She is to be my student, and her name is Mary Anne Satterwhite.

The Satterwhite name was already well known to me. I would see Mr. Satterwhite, Mary Anne's father, whenever I went downtown to "his bank," to make a deposit or to cash a check. And Mary Anne's brother Bill, several years her senior, had been my student in English for four semesters. Bill was already on the way to becoming a doctor, and many of us who admire him, including myself, are grateful that he brought to Winston-Salem his exceptional skills in medicine, as well as the compassion and integrity that have defined his life.

Like Bill, Mary Anne was my student for four semesters, two in the town of Wake Forest and two in Winston-Salem. She then became, a little later, my teaching assistant. (By the way, between Bill and Mary Anne, I also taught a student named Doug Maynard. The circle of friendship thus became beautifully complete. In those days at Wake Forest there was truly "splendour in the grass" and "glory in the flower.")

Mary Anne, like Bill and Doug, had all the talents and determination to become a professional woman in whatever field she might have chosen. She was an all-A student. But a few months before graduation she responded with a happy "yes" to a proposal from Doug, and a different career opened for her. It would be commonplace to say that she chose marriage and motherhood before the fulfillment of intellectual ambitions; I prefer to say that she chose family adventure rather than the routine of office and laboratory: the adventures that, every day, her children – and, later, her grandchildren – invited her to plan and to realize; the adventures she shared here in Winston-Salem with a galaxy of friends who sought her company and her counsel; the adventures that carried her around the world to more destinations, near and far, than I can name or imagine. Her immersion in a life lived fully every day was more to be treasured by her, I would suggest, than any formal advanced studies she might have sought. She created a home where the fruits of the mind and the spirit were constantly in evidence and where a hopeful and progressive outlook on the larger world was manifested any time that family and friends gathered.

Mary Anne and Doug Maynard at Wake Forest's combined college and medical school graduation in 1959

The poet Wordsworth, whose life was blessed by his marriage of forty-eight years and by his five children, wrote about the young woman he met and married: "She was a Phantom of delight / When first she gleamed upon my sight; / A lovely Apparition, sent / To be a moment's ornament." Later, in marriage, the poet husband learned to notice more and more "Her household motions light and free … A countenance in which did meet / Sweet records, promises as sweet." In still later years, as time passed, he saw her as "A perfect woman, nobly planned, … And yet a Spirit still and bright / With something of angelic light."

As a complement to Wordsworth's poem about his wife, I would like to recall the New England poet Anne Bradstreet's poem about her husband:

If ever two were one, then surely we.
If ever man were lov'd by wife, then thee;
If ever wife was happy in a man,
Compare with me ye women if you can.
I prize thy love more than whole Mines of gold,
Or all the riches that the East doth hold.

In the last few weeks, as I have talked with friends of Mary Anne and Doug, one theme has been constant: how much Mary Anne and Doug loved each other, how much they depended on each other, how much they inspired each other. "If ever two were one, then surely they."

Today we remember Mary Anne from different perspectives: Doug, each of the children, each of the grandchildren, each friend has a particular, unforgettable picture of her. Mine comes from more than fifty years ago. Yours probably comes from more recent years: from a shared meal, a casual conversation, a momentary glimpse of her smile or her kindness. These memories are all true, and together they constitute her legacy to us. If we could recount them all, as of course one person cannot, we would see her in all her richness, and we would be newly thankful that she was our friend.

Last month Mary Anne celebrated her 75th birthday, and she wrote, "I've always loved celebrating birthdays." What she really meant, I think, was that she loved celebrating life.

A recent memory that I have of Mary Anne comes from a Saturday morning at the Farmers' Market, two or three months ago. I did not know then that she was ill. But, as I spoke to her, I saw once again the face of a college freshman: beautiful, bright, and happy; the beauty, the brightness, the happiness were still there. They are still there with us this morning.

October 26, 2013

Cyclone Covey

History Faculty

No one who ever met Cyclone Covey will forget him. It was as if his whole body was somehow responding to the energy of his lively mind: he not only looked at you in a penetrating way; he took in your whole being. Even his eyebrows danced. You were cast under his spell, and in the minutes that followed you might learn what you did not know about a wide variety of subjects – from the poetry of Emily Dickinson to Roger Williams and the Pilgrims to a Roman Jewish colony in America at the time of Charlemagne.

Many – perhaps most – scholars in the academic world choose one country, one century, one person, one theme as their own and donate their careers with increasing precision to the particular subject that claims their working allegiance. Cyclone believed that history includes everything – is everything – and his mind raced across countries, across centuries, across causes, across people. Along the way he listened to music: its stories, its sounds, its harmonies, its transcendence. I would not be surprised if he heard the music of the spheres.

When Cyclone and Bonnie and their children came to Wake Forest in

1968 to join the history department, they were following another animating, sometimes enigmatic personality: James Ralph Scales, who had recently brought his family to Winston-Salem to take up his new post as the eleventh president of Wake Forest. Every person who came east with Scales brought something of the robust pioneering spirit of Oklahoma, and that spirit mixed with what was – at least until recently – the progressive spirit of North Carolina to create, I would suggest, a unique chapter in Wake Forest history that remains vivid to all of us who remember its charm and its character. Those recruits from Oklahoma had both style and substance.

It was not long after Cyclone arrived that he discovered another original personality: Nicholas Bragg, the creative director of Reynolda House. Isn't it fascinating to imagine the two of them meeting for the first time? For eighteen summers, with other men and women of learning that Nick recruited, they offered American Foundations seminars to students of all ages, especially teachers seeking to advance their knowledge in music, art, literature, and history.

Even today, when American Foundations alumni get together, they talk about the "good old days" at Reynolda House. Nick says that Cyclone was at the heart of that program, awakening minds and spreading a gospel of radical belief.

The last time I saw Cyclone – several weeks ago – it was where I almost always saw him: in the Library. He was there with Julie, and he was on the search for I know not what: something, I suppose, that would defy my own provincial understanding. Nick Bragg, who for years regularly visited Cyclone, has a more poignant memory of his "last time" with Cyclone. He saw him, ten days ago, at Baptist Hospital. In Nick's own words, "I called his name from the hall, and Cyclone said in a happy voice, 'Ah, Nicholas, I am getting stronger every day.'"

Those words – "I am getting stronger every day" – are a provocative key to the way in which Cyclone Covey lived life: "Excelsior! Ever onward!" This afternoon we honor him with our gratitude, and also salute his wife Bonnie, who was always at his side, carving out a niche of her own in college and community women's organizations and becoming a force for good in a world that, more than ever, needs people like Bonnie and Cyclone Covey.

December 1, 2013

Lee Potter

English Faculty

WHY WAS LEE POTTER so widely admired, and why do we remember him with such affection?

To meet Lee, even for the first time, was to like him. His good looks (of course), his courtliness, his charm brought instant attention.

And every later encounter with Lee renewed that first impression. Not long after he arrived at Wake Forest – almost half a century ago – he became the man in the English department most loved – especially, I think, by young newcomers who found in him a sympathetic listener and a wise and patient guide through the troublesome crises of academic life.

And so it was with students: good students who glistened with success and somewhat lesser students who struggled to learn. Lee's pleasure in the company of students was vividly on display in Venice and in London, where, on five different occasions, he and Edith lived for a semester in a College house with 15 or 20 students, prepared meals with them, counseled them, walked with them, showed them the sights of the cities, and shared with them the excitement of being abroad.

One former student from the London house recalls that "his twinkling eyes often belied his seemingly ironic perspectives." "I spent a semester," she says, "trying to figure out when he was serious and when he was making kind fun of something."

Whether abroad or at home, Lee had the perfect companion in Edith. She brought into his life – and into our lives as well – a full measure of grace and the sounds of music, heard and unheard. In their Winston-Salem home they entertained guests in a style uncommon at Wake Forest. This afternoon, in my mind's eye, I see the Potters' living room, their dinner table, their pianos – and I also see visitors from abroad (V.S. Pritchett and Stephen Spender), from elsewhere in America (Malcolm Cowley, and, memorably, James Dickey), and, often, just plain folks like you and me.

Lee was – and has often been called – a Southern gentleman. And he was, unmistakably, a gentleman with Southern manners. But to call him mainly Southern is to diminish his universality. He loved colleagues and students, wherever they came from, and he loved life, wherever it took him. And I think he also loved us, even when he was amused by us. If he were here with us today, as of old, he would smile, eyes sparkling, observe all that is said and done, recall something out of literature to interpret the occasion, have

thoughts perhaps unspoken, and tell us all to look around and relax. His contagious spirit would – as always in the past – be our guide toward a satisfying day.

January 28, 2014

Herman Preseren
Education Faculty

N OT HAVING ATTENDED one of Herman Preseren's classes, I cannot speak about him as a teacher. And, not having lived in that faculty enclave at the east end of Faculty Drive, I cannot speak about him as a close neighbor. My experiences with Herman – and therefore my views of him – were shaped from a different perspective, the perspective of a friend and colleague who knew and observed him not so much as a Professor of Education but simply as a person, as a very fine human being.

Why was he, I have asked myself in remembering him – why was he a fine human being? What do I think of – what do other friends think of – when we think of Herman Preseren?

I think of his friendliness, his graciousness, his smile – his greeting which was always full of kindness. Whether in Tribble Hall, at home or church or professional meeting, or, I am sure, on some distant street in France or England or Germany, he was always the polite gentleman. I almost said "Southern gentleman," because, even though he was born and grew up and went to college in Pennsylvania, he had what some of us provincial Southerners like to think of as Southern charm. Maybe we can give the credit to his many years at Wake Forest, but I suspect the credit goes simply to him (and probably his parents) and to an innate courtesy that his years in North Carolina only added to and strengthened.

I think also of his versatility. As one who has always been clumsy with any machine more complicated than a wind-up watch or an old-fashioned camera, I marveled at Herman's skills with instruments, gadgets, mechanical equipment of all kinds. He was at home with all those devices that record, and make it possible for us to remember, the lives we have lived – whether athletic events or trips to Europe or just the miscellaneous sights and sounds of our everyday, shared experiences. I saluted him for the way in which he moved as comfortably among things as he did among human beings. I suspect that he was polite to them too.

I think also of Herman's courage and his patience. I guess these were life long qualities, but, as we all know, they became most visible immediately after that accident – an accident that would have crushed not only the body but also the spirit of a person less invincible than Herman. We watched him recover and grow strong again, and we became freshly aware of his extraordinary determination and his sensitive – all the more sensitive, perhaps, because it was understated – love of life. In William Faulkner's words, Herman not only "endured"; he "prevailed."

Years ago, Professor Jasper Memory said to me, "Herman Preseren is a man of impeccable character." I suppose, finally, that, when I think of Herman, I think of his character – his honesty, his selflessness, his spiritual wholeness. I believe that he knew who he was.

In a passage from Shakespeare's *Henry V* that I have always liked, the young King of England, trying to win the heart of a French princess, says that, of all the qualities a man might possess, the best is "a good heart." "A good heart," says Henry, "is the sun and the moon; or rather the sun, and not the moon, for it shines bright and never changes, but keeps his course truly."

Herman had that "good heart." He shone bright, and never changed, and kept his course truly. We remember him with respect and love.

May 17, 2014

Maya Angelou

Reynolds Professor of American Studies

Also speaking at Dr. Angelou's service were former President Bill Clinton and First Lady, Michelle Obama.

I WANT TO SPEAK particularly this morning to those of you who are experiencing Wake Forest for the first time. We are happy that for these hours in Wait Chapel you are part of Maya Angelou's Wake Forest family, and we hope that you will be inspired by your visit to come again.

WFU Reynolds Professor of American Studies Dr. Maya Angelou speaks to the WFU Law School during National Banned Books Week.

Maya Angelou brought distinction and her unique grandeur to her thirty-two years at Wake Forest. But – in a quieter way – she was, perhaps most of all, an always generous neighbor and friend, responding to every request for a speech, an interview, or a conversation with someone who wanted to meet her. We know that Maya Angelou "belonged" to America, and indeed she "belonged" to the world, but we like to think that in a special way she "belonged" first – after her family – to Wake Forest. We were grateful that, on the day after she received from President Obama the Presidential Medal of Freedom, she proudly said to a Washington audience, "I am a Wake Forest woman. You can't beat that."

So today we cherish the remarkable story of an enormously gifted woman who would have been welcome anywhere in the land but who chose – I think because she knew that besides honoring her, we loved her and wanted her as a companion – to come to this Southern university and make it her home for the rest of her life. At Wake Forest she found a new career: "I'm not a writer who teaches," she said. "I'm a teacher who writes." And until her last day she continued to write and to teach and to bless us with her presence.

Maya Angelou has become part of the history and the fabric of Wake Forest, dazzlingly and forever.

Her legacy lives on at Wake Forest: Maya Angelou Hall was dedicated in February 2017.

June 7, 2014

Penelope Niven

Graduate School Alumna, Biographer

WHEN I BECAME PENELOPE Niven's friend in the autumn months of 1961 – in the Library classroom where I was teaching – I knew, from all that I saw in her, that her life after Wake Forest would be productive and rewarding. She had academic skills that pointed naturally toward a career in teaching and writing. She had a clear and perceptive understanding of herself. And she had a winsomeness and charm that made her memorably appealing. Anyone who saw her once wanted to see her again.

But what neither I nor anyone, I think, could have foreseen in her school days was that she would become a biographer of rare distinction and that her subjects would include a poet of the Midwestern prairies, an African-American actor of Broadway and Hollywood, a sophisticated photographer, and a writer whose plays and novels have become an enduring part of the fabric of American literature. Penny did tell me once that the biographical episodes in Romantic poetry that we read together – as, for example, in Wordsworth's *Prelude* and Byron's *Childe Harold's Pilgrimage* – did have a special appeal for her.

But her own mid-life years of discovery and maturity and her abiding interest in other people were the primary sources of the understanding – and impeccable taste – she brought to her talent as a biographer. And to that task, moreover, she showed a determination and a commitment that took her to what must have seemed never-ending hours in libraries, in interviews, and in travels to whatever places promised new insights into her theme. She seemed tireless.

The last time I saw Penny, she was as beautiful as ever. She was ready to begin new projects. She spoke with her familiar tenderness about Jennifer. And she was happy.

At the conclusion of William Wordsworth's magnificent autobiography, he looks to future writers, as Penny did, and says,

we to them will speak
A lasting inspiration…
What we have loved,
Others will love, and we will teach them how;
Instruct them how the mind of man becomes
A thousand times more beautiful than the earth
… In beauty exalted, as it is itself
Of quality and fabric more divine.

To Wordsworth's words – inspiration, beauty, love – Penny Niven would have added the word "joy."

September 8, 2014

Ed Christman

Alumnus, Chaplain
Received the Medallion of Merit in 2007

Ed, and his wife, Jean, in their front yard in 2008, having discovered their front yard rolled in honor of his birthday.

These remarks were given on the occasion of his retirement in 2003.

IN ONE SCENE OF JIM DODDING'S exhilarating production of *The Servant of Two Masters*, a member of a merry dancing troupe calls out "Waiter." No one appears. Then she yells, "Landlord." Still no one comes. Finally she shouts, "Anybody." This time, to the surprise of everyone in the audience, Ed Christman emerges from behind a door: a white-haired Venetian named Cameriere within the context of the play, but obviously, to those who know, the Chaplain himself.

Edwin G. Wilson | 127

Thus, last week, did Ed Christman give us a cameo performance in an unlikely and unexpected place, recalling his appearances in earlier seasons as God in the *Passion Play* – type casting, some people said – and as Arvide Abernathy in *Guys and Dolls*, tenderly singing – singing, no less! –"More I cannot wish you than to wish you find your love, Your own true love this day."

Ed Christman gladly accepts such small roles on the Wake Forest main stage and interprets them in his own inimitable way, but offstage he is more often seen as a major supporting actor, wisely and generously giving guidance and friendship to the stars of the occasion: a young man and a young woman planning their wedding, a student confused about the direction and purpose of his life, another student confronting despair or rejection, a faculty member injured or ill and facing uncertain recovery, parents whose son or daughter has been killed or is dying.

Fortunately, more often than not, the scene is a happier one: a moment of success or triumph or reconciliation. Either way, Ed is on call; he is available; he is there; through his words, through his quiet and patient presence, he gives support.

Working on his character for HMS Pinafore

Ed is also a director. Week after week he is responsible for a morning chapel service, and every fall he plans the several days of a pre-school retreat, designed from his own original blueprint. The setting is a camp in the country; the atmosphere is relaxed; the cast of speakers have been recruited from here and there on campus; the audience is made up largely of students who are new to Wake Forest and who have come to the retreat expectantly and eagerly. They will have their first taste of what being a college student means, and guiding them through this first act of their Wake Forest lives will be the director Ed Christman.

My own first memory of Ed Christman takes me back to a classroom in Wait Hall on the old campus where perhaps fifteen or twenty people were planning what was then called "Religious Emphasis Week." I was a novice faculty member, and Ed was an undergraduate. Who else was there I cannot say, but Ed is the one I remember. Why? I'm not sure, but I think it was the way he listened, the conciliatory way in which he spoke, his attentiveness to everyone, his somehow conveying the impression – a correct impression – that he had a personal commitment of some kind that was larger than the details of our discussion.

That meeting was more than fifty years ago. I was not sure at that time that I would stay at Wake Forest, though I hoped I would, and I could not have foreseen that "after many wanderings, many years of absence" Ed would come back, also to stay. But I knew that Ed – besides having a gift for small but significant gestures and in addition to showing talents for supporting and directing – was destined to become a star.

Rev. Ed Christman receives his Medallion of Merit at Founder's Day Convocation in 2007.

Since 1969 – as Chaplain of Wake Forest University – Ed has been that "star" – a star in one of the longest-running shows Wake Forest has produced. Ed, of course, is a Baptist – if I may say so, in the best sense of that sometimes exalted and sometimes maligned word – and he has ministered in a brotherly way to the Baptist Student Union, to Poteat Scholars, and to others who live within the oldest of Wake Forest's religious families.

'Brother Ed' conducts his last regular chapel service in Wait Chapel on Thursday, April 24, 2003 - retiring after 49 years of service to the university.

But he has been a Chaplain to everybody – to those of other faiths, to those of no faith, to those on the road somewhere. And I have known – and still know – students and professors, disposed not to like – certainly not to accept – chaplains in general, who have none the less found Ed Christman a friend whom they could respect and honor and trust. They know that he loves them, whoever they are or whatever they believe.

When one faculty member was asked what he wanted in our next chaplain, he said, "A clone of Ed Christman." Wake Forest will doubtless find a splendid new chaplain, but, I must say, he (or she) will not be another Ed Christman. There is no other Ed Christman. Ed stands apart. He is unique. We of a Wake Forest world which is now drifting into memory are blessed to have known him and to have been his friend.

April 16, 2003 (Retirement Celebration)
December 30, 2014 (Memorial Service)

Eunice Johnson
My Assistant in the Provost's Office

Many of you knew Eunice Johnson in her home, in her neighborhood, at church, in the public schools, around town – wherever the activities and the friendships of her long and happy life of one hundred years took her. She was a wise and gentle woman, unfailingly polite, lovingly attentive to home and hearth and family, bringing good will wherever she went, and blessed with a quick wit that kept people relaxed and smiling.

I knew her in a different setting. For twenty years or so, she was my secretary, my assistant, in the Dean's – and then the Provost's – office at Wake Forest. Our day together typically began at 8:30 in the morning and ended at 5:00 in the afternoon. We had many visitors: some who came just to say hello, others who were looking for information, others who simply wanted to talk, occasionally those who wanted to complain. They were professors, members of the staff.

I have one memory which I particularly treasure. She found out that my favorite dessert is coconut cake, and her Christmas gift to me was a delicious coconut cake, the best I ever knew. Every year, after she retired, and as recently as last Christmas, she would bake a coconut cake for me and bring it to my house on Christmas Eve, along with a tin of comparably delicious buttermints. I came to expect – and I was never disappointed – that just after dark, on December 24, I would hear a car in the driveway, I would go out and see Mrs. Johnson, usually with Sarah (who had become her assistant cook), with mints and a coconut cake, and I would take the cake to where my family was waiting. They knew what to expect. They knew it was a highlight of Christmas.

June 11, 2015

Jack Williams
Physics Faculty

I N EVERY GENERATION of college professors there are a few men and women who go beyond what is expected of them as teachers and scholars and embrace the entire institution and the larger nearby community.

One such person was Jack Williams, who, from 1958 on, was a valued physicist who sought every opportunity to strengthen the Department and give direction to its future. On faculty committees and faculty councils he listened patiently to all points of view, thought wisely about what was best for Wake Forest and then acted judiciously. It helped, of course, in all such meetings, that he was enormously likable and that he immediately inspired trust.

I particularly treasure one experience I shared with Jack. He and I went to New York for a few days to meet with the head of the Olin Foundation to talk about a physics building. Physics was crowded with chemistry in Salem Hall and, rather desperately, needed space for clasrooms, offices and laboratories. The Olin Foundation sometimes gave entire buildings to colleges, and Jack thought hopefully that the Foundation might be willing to hear about Wake Forest. We were given an opportunity to make our case, and Jack did so brilliantly – with historical data, with facts, with what could be accomplished in a new building – and, of course, with personal charm. His presentation, as we now know, succeeded, and Wake Forest physics acquired an entire building all to itself: the only instance I know of in which one academic department – incidentally, without significant support from the Development staff – met with such resounding success. We should remember Jack for that achievement. And, by the way, he and I had a good time in New York: we had at least two excellent meals, and we saw one Broadway play.

Dr. Williams animates his physics lecture.

At home, on Faculty Drive, Jack and Mitzi were thoughtful and generous neighbors, and they brought to all of us a sense of rootedness, of well being. I have always thought of a faculty community as ideally incorporating wives, husbands, children, grandchildren, all the neighbors; the Williams family was an integral part of our lives. As an English teacher I am not qualified to speak of Jack as a physicist, and I am not a golfer, but I remember Jack gratefully as a man of conscience and vision who was faithful to the ideals that gave birth to Wake Forest and who brought strength wherever and whenever he could.

November 12, 2015

Marcellus Waddill

Mathematics Faculty

As an English major, in my long-ago undergraduate days at Wake Forest, I took the required courses in algebra and trigonometry, but I went no further. Calculus still remains unknown to me, and words like "Fibonacci," for instance, were – and are – totally outside my vocabulary. So, as I come here today to memorialize Marcellus Waddill, I realize that I cannot tell you from personal insights about Marcellus as a mathematician or as a teacher of mathematics. I have heard from others about his professional strengths, his effectiveness in the classroom, and his leadership in the Department, which one colleague, John Baxley, has described as "calm, completely fair, always courteous and without harsh words, always seeking for compromise and cordiality." But I must look at Marcellus from a somewhat different perspective: from outside the Department and the classroom; and see him as a man of the best Wake Forest traditions whose character, whose values, whose "honor" – that was an important word to him – colored and shaped everything he did and said. He was predictably conservative, in the best sense of the word, and he resisted any challenge to what he saw as an affront to the integrity of Wake Forest or to its historic ideals. As an administrator and as a friend, I knew I could count on Marcellus to speak the unvarnished truth.

Marcellus' students – from all that I have heard – have doubtless profited from what he taught them about mathematics, but they will, I think, mainly retain in their hearts and memories what he exemplified as a man. It is important to remember that the campus-wide Wake Forest awards he received during his career here were for his community service, for his contributions to student life, and for his excellence in advising.

Marcellus himself gracefully recognized his students as the centerpiece of his 35 years at Wake Forest. "Teaching," he said, "was the most important thing I did – the most important thing we all do. That's what made my experience at Wake Forest a happy one."

So, I think, it is to Marcellus' students that we must look as we seek to define the true legacy of what he himself called his "happy" career. One group of students, in particular, have remained steadfast and loyal to Marcellus through all the years: the members of the Sigma Chi fraternity, to whom he was a faithful faculty advisor and friend. One of those devoted disciples, Ed Hallman, recently wrote to me. "Marcellus blessed us with his presence, comforted us in our losses, and stood beside us when we experienced our success and also when we failed, always loving us and teaching us to live and grow while embracing the ideals of brotherhood which we shared with him. Each of us is a better person for having known him. Each of us has been blessed by his profound influence for good in our lives and in particular by his example of Christian love and stewardship. Marcellus gave us the gift of his truly good heart."

What more ennobling tribute could a college professor – or any man or woman – receive? And the rest of us, in less creative ways, can also say, "Yes, this is the Marcellus Waddill we knew, and we are grateful for his character, his exemplary service, and his friendship." Certainly, I can say this morning for myself that Marcellus, on numerous occasions, shared with me his vision, his ideals and his strength, and I, like so many of you, consider myself fortunate to have known him and to have been his friend. I will remember what he taught by his example, and, as a long-time Wake Forester, must say that I hope that what Marcellus Waddill stood for will always, as the years come and go, be at the heart of our University's commitments and mission: It may be more important than anything else.

August 27, 2016

Clara and Charles Allen

Clara Allen

Singer, Wife of Professor Charles Allen

I BEGIN WITH VERSES from the 98th Psalm:

> O sing unto the Lord a new song; for he hath done marvellous things: his right hand, and his holy arm, hath gotten him the victory.
> Make a joyful noise unto the Lord, all the earth: make a loud noise, and rejoice, and sing praise.
> Sing unto the Lord with the harp; with the harp, and the voice of a psalm.
> With trumpets and sound of cornet make a joyful noise before the Lord, the King.
> Let the sea roar, and the fullness thereof; the world, and they that dwell therein.
> Let the floods clap their hands: let the hills be joyful together
> Before the Lord; for he cometh to judge the earth: with righteousness shall he judge the world, and the people with equity.

One spring afternoon, when I was a student on the old, the original campus of Wake Forest, I was sitting on the front porch of Mrs. Fannie Gorrell's house on Faculty Avenue. My friend, Charlie Allen, at that time an instructor in biology, came by to say hello. With him was a beautiful young woman whom he introduced as his girlfriend, Clara. After a few words of getting acquainted, Charlie said, "Clara is a singer." I said to Clara, "Won't you sing something?" And, rather surprisingly to me, she did sing: a song, called "My Hero," from an operetta "The Chocolate Soldier." Everything about her – her looks, her voice, her gracious manner – captivated me. And my admiration for her, beginning that long ago afternoon in old Wake Forest, has remained from that day on.

Clara had a way of understanding and absorbing a song – its words, its tones, its reason for being – and caressing it; so that, when you heard her sing, you knew that she was authentic and that there was something both musically rich and engagingly human in her voice and in her personality.

Those same qualities appeared for me – over and over again – when I came as a guest to her home on Faculty Drive. I don't know how many of you were here during what I remember as a Golden Age of musical performances at Wake Forest, when Charlie directed the Artists Series and he and Clara entertained famously talented guests from around the world. If you doubt my memories, look back at a list of who came to Wake Forest during the Allen years. The Allens' home was always alive with food and spirit appropriate to the occasion. And Clara was in our midst: charming, enthusiastic, and welcoming to one and all.

The poet Shelley wrote "Music, when soft voices die, vibrates in the memory." Today, I am sure, Clara and her music vibrate collectively and individually in our memory, and we continue, in our memory, to be blessed.

I conclude with verses from Paul's letter to the Colossians:

Let the word of Christ dwell in you richly in all wisdom; teaching and admonishing one another in psalms and hymns and spiritual songs, singing with grace in your hearts to the Lord.

And whatsoever ye do in word or deed, do all in the name of the Lord Jesus, giving thanks to God and the Father by him.

September 9, 2017

From left: Professors Harold Tedford and Don Wolfe in the foyer of the Main Stage Theatre in Scales Fine Arts Center
Inset: Jim Dodding

Don Wolfe

Theatre Faculty

TODAY WE REMEMBER and celebrate a talented and lovable man who, with two other men of purpose and achievement, created a tradition of excellence in the story of the Wake Forest Theatre.

In recent weeks those of you who are in theatre and those of us who simply love the theatre have honored the memory of Jim Dodding, the brilliant Englishman whose musical theatre, we all agreed, was beyond compare.

On another occasion, we saw the dedication of the mainstage theatre to our teacher and friend Harold Tedford: always friendly, always available for talk.

Today we salute Don Wolfe, who came here in 1968 – three years after Harold had arrived – to teach, to direct, and to inspire us. 51 years among us: always courteous, always kind, always insightful, a patient listener. How many times have he and Harold and I had lunch together? And I think I saw almost every play that Don directed.

Don Wolfe, Harold Tedford, Jim Dodding: those three men who gave us a legacy that has made the Wake Forest theatre a place of quality and of excitement. We give thanks to them all.

And their legacy continues today – in a somewhat different form. We see talented women at the heart of the theatre. They and their male colleagues are preserving the legacy they inherited, and every year their productions "light up the sky" just as those of their predecessors did.

I chose to offer my remarks in this fashion, because Don, a man of modesty and good humor, would, I thought, be happy with the approach I have taken and because I love this theatre with passion and consider the Wake Forest theatre a cherished treasure of the best of Wake Forest life.

Don, we are today what you have helped in so many ways to create. I greet you and bless you on this memorial afternoon of gratitude and remembrance.

April 27, 2019

The Essence of Wake Forest

WHEN I BEGIN TO THINK of the Wake Forest I know and love, two words come at once to my mind: friendliness and honor. I heard them for the first time as Wake Forest words on the night of my own freshman orientation. "At Wake Forest," Professor Jasper Memory said, "You say hello to everyone you meet." (Memory: What a great name for a college professor!) And Pete Davis, the president of the student body, told us about the honor system: "We do not use proctors. We trust you. Just sign your name. That's enough." And – for many years – every Wake Forest freshman was given a badge to wear. The badge had two words on it: friendliness and honor.

Wearing his badge, Freshman James Dozier shakes hands with Professor Memory.

The friendliness we spoke of was not just about saying "Good morning" or waving a hand in greeting. Nor was it merely a sign of Southern hospitality or student camaraderie. It incorporated the faculty also. The student yearbook, in fact, introduced the faculty section with the words "Our Friends the Faculty." And beyond the Monday, Wednesday, and Friday classes and the Tuesday and Thursday afternoon laboratories, where teaching and learning officially took place, there were frequent encounters between students and teachers – here

Edwin G. Wilson | 139

and there on the campus or in town – which opened eyes and inspired confidence and led to new insights about one's life and career.

One night, for example, I was studying physics and needed to learn about the Wheatstone bridge. I saw that my professor, Bill Speas, was in his office, and I went by to ask for help. He was in a chair at his desk, listening to a record being played on an old department turntable. Before I could inquire about the Wheatstone bridge, he invited me to sit down and said, "Listen to this!" Then I heard, for the first time, "Che gelida manina," from *La Bohème*, sung by the Pavarotti of his day, the great Italian tenor, Beniamino Gigli. To this day I could not explain the Wheatstone bridge to you, but I could, if called upon, hum my way through that aria by Puccini.

The English novelist, E.M. Forster, once wrote about Cambridge, his college, trying to capture what he calls the magic quality of college life. He said that at Cambridge "Body and spirit, reason and emotion, work and play, architecture and scenery, laughter and seriousness, life and art – these pairs which are elsewhere contrasted – were fused into one. People and books reinforced one another, intelligence joined hands with affection, speculation became a passion, and discussion was made profound by love." In this way, he said, the university "became for a moment universal."

I do not wish to make unsupported claims for Wake Forest or for our faculty, but I do believe that "friendliness" between students and teachers is still part of our collegiate environment. The other day, I received, as I often do, a letter from a recent graduate. This one said: "I've told many folks that, if I had to make my college decision over 100 times, I would 100 times choose Wake Forest. It was a perfect setting for a young man from the rural environment of Anson County who wanted to broaden his horizons. Upon arrival I found myself woefully unprepared academically but also at once I found the opportunity [to learn and grow]." He then mentioned by name ten professors – from seven different departments – who had helped and inspired him.

Perhaps a better word than "friendliness" is "friendship." I think that Wake Forest is a place for friendship. And, when I look at the two words we have chosen to define the Wake Forest faculty member – teacher and scholar – I speculate that maybe we should add a third word: friend. That may well be the best word of all.

Toward the end of his life the Irish poet William Butler Yeats walked through an art gallery in Dublin and looked at the portraits hanging on the wall. Some of them were of his friends, and he reminisced about them. Yeats was, by then, probably the greatest living poet in the English language, winner of the Nobel Prize for Literature, a member of the Senate of the Irish Free State. And yet, as he, looking at pictures, came to the end of his thoughts, he said:

Think where man's glory most begins and ends
And say my glory was I had such friends.

So, on that first night of my own orientation, Wake Forest said to me, "Friendliness." Wake Forest also said to me, "Honor." That word invited me into a community of good will where people trusted one another and where other related words – "moral," "ethical," "spiritual" – were central to our education. For some modern academicians these words are fraught with peril – their fear is that in academe we might, if we talk about morality, go beyond the borders of rationalism and objectivity – but my own Wake Forest heritage obliges me to confront these words.

To that end I will go back to what is perhaps the greatest address ever delivered at Harvard University: by Ralph Waldo Emerson in 1837. It was called "The American Scholar" and it was Emerson's challenge to each of his listeners to be what he called "Man Thinking." (Note the words "Scholar" and "Thinking") But even though Emerson's theme was "Man Thinking," he said, "Character is higher than intellect." "Thinking" is only "a partial act." "Let the grandeur of justice shine in [your] affairs. Let the beauty of affection cheer [your] lowly roof." [Hear that word "affection" again!] "Nothing can bring you peace but the triumph of principles."

As I look at our nation, at our world, as they appear today, I see an increasingly urgent opportunity – and need – for men and women like Wake Forest students – who, to be sure, in Emerson's word, "think" but also represent character, affection, justice, principle. I would say indeed that principles are more important to our students – and, of course, to us too – than high grades or intellect, as valuable as they are. Almost every day, it seems – in newspapers or on television – we read about someone – an athlete, a writer, a professor, a banker, a businessman, a candidate for office, a governor, a Congressman, a minister, a priest – a person of presumed intellect – a person who thinks – who none the less – led by thoughtless passion, by selfishness, by greed – turns away from family, friends, and obligations and betrays a public trust. Almost every failure we hear about – almost every fall from grace – whether in Raleigh or in Washington or on Wall Street or even sometimes in our home towns – is a moral failure, not an intellectual failure. And these failures, unfortunately, are bipartisan and interfaith, and they ignore Emerson's warning: "Nothing can bring you peace but the triumph of principles."

Obviously, the Wake Forest concept of "honor" was rooted in the Christian faith and, specifically, in that version of Christian faith that is called "Baptist." But Wake Forest, even on the old campus, was not imprisoned by creed or doctrine, nor was the classroom used as a setting for persuasion toward belief. Religion was prevalent as an assumption but not a proclamation. Evidences of faith were all around us, but they were, so to speak, between the lines. I took religion courses in the "teachings of Jesus" and the "teachings of Paul," but my teacher, a distinguished ordained Baptist minister, taught the Gospels and the Epistles by using essentially the same method by which, in a government course, I was being taught the Federalist papers and, in an English course, I was reading Shakespeare's sonnets. My philosophy professor, a man of renowned piety, taught me Nietzsche ("Haven't you heard that God is dead"?), and in a class on the modern novel, my English teacher required us to read Virginia Woolf, D.H. Lawrence, and James Joyce's *Ulysses*: books that, in the early 1940s, were not often included in a college's English curriculum.

These three men I speak of – my religion professor, my philosophy professor, and my English professor – were all, typically, to be seen on Sunday morning, worshipping at the campus Baptist church. They saw – and I saw – no limit to the search for truth – what Harvard chose to call "Veritas" – even in the context of what were still unmistakably Baptist commitments. They showed that moral and ethical, even religious, commitments can be combined with the highest academic standards.

The story of Wake Forest since 1834 has parallels almost everywhere in private higher education in America. Until 1843 the motto of Harvard, then two centuries old, was "Christo et Ecclesiae": "For Christ and the Church." Only then was the motto changed to

"Veritas": "Truth." Wake Forest's motto of "Pro Humanitate" did not require such a radical change; it simply had to be reinterpreted. Originally, "Pro Humanitate" was meant to echo the words of Jesus to his disciples: "Go into all the world and proclaim the good news to the whole creation." "And the disciples went out and proclaimed the good news everywhere." Today, "Pro Humanitate" is still Wake Forest's much cherished motto, and the original interpretation is still being heard by some who wish to "proclaim" the good news of the Gospels, but it is no longer for most Wake Foresters an invitation to proclaim and to convert. Rather it tells us to be friends to all humanity with honor, to teach, to help, to serve. And nothing is more encouraging to me than to know students and alumni who hear the words "Pro Humanitate" and then, with friendship and honor, put those words into practice.

As we look to the future, I hope that we will remember "friendliness" and "honor" and "Pro Humanitate" as cornerstones of what I think of as the uniqueness of Wake Forest as a university. I do not like to talk about "peer institutions," and may I say that for me national rankings of universities are invariably shallow and partial and not to be trusted. Wake Forest really has no "peers." There is no other school quite like us. We stand alone. We are what we are. We do not exist in relation to other schools; we succeed or we fail only in so far as we are true to our commitments, to our own ambitions, to our own destiny, to friendship and honor. Let me illustrate what I mean.

In athletics we are fond of praising our uniqueness. No other school in the Atlantic Coast Conference (the eight public universities and the three other quite different private universities), we say, is quite like Wake Forest. And our athletic directors of the past century – Jim Weaver, Gene Hooks, and Ron Wellman – have built admirably successful programs not by imitating some other school or by following a generic model, but through creativity and with a recognition that there are certain principles beyond athletics that athletics, like every other division in the University, must adhere to. I would hope that all our other programs could be uniquely Wake Forest in that same way. Let us, as we move toward our goal of being – in Wake Forest's President Nathan Hatch's words – "a collegiate university," be not just one among many but, at heart, the same Wake Forest we have always been.

If I have any anxiety about Wake Forest's future, it is that, because of the increasingly high cost of a Wake Forest education, we can not enroll young men and women who want to come to Wake Forest, who have all the necessary credentials, who are of good character and purpose, but who do not have the money that is required. Many of us are fortunate, and I hope that Wake Forest will some day admit my grandchildren, but I also want to see in our student body the children either of parents who did not go to college or of parents whose resources are modest and severely limited. Such students would come to Wake Forest – without a background of privilege, without any sense of entitlement, without arrogance – they would, I think, come eager, hopeful, hungry, ready to broaden their horizons – like the young man form the rural environment of Anson Country I spoke of earlier – and they would often become the kind of Wake Forest students whom we have always honored and cherished and taken delight in, and around whom the words "friendliness" and "honor" were first woven. So, I think we should plan "financial aid for students" at the very heart of our institutional endeavors. Only then, I think, will our future be what our past has destined it to be. Only then can we fully declare our embracing friendliness and our steadfast honor. Only then can "Pro Humanitate" – for all humanity – remain truly our motto.

Because I have talked at length about friendliness and honor and may seem to have ignored the academic purposes which, after all, give substance to a university, I want to end with a tribute to learning itself. It comes from T.H. White's *The Sword in the Stone*, a retelling of the legend of King Arthur. (You may have read it when you were a boy or a girl.) The wise old magician Merlin is giving his student, the once and future King Arthur, some farewell advice about how he should use his time. "The best thing," says Merlin, "is to learn something. That is the only thing that never fails. You may grow old and trembling...you may lie awake at night...you may miss your only love, you may see the world about you devastated by evil lunatics, [you may see] your honor trampled in the sewers of baser minds. There is only one thing for it then – to learn.... That is the only thing which the mind can never exhaust, never alienate, never be tortured by, never fear or distrust, and never dream of regretting. Learning is the thing for you. Look at what a lot of things there are to learn – pure science,… astronomy,… natural history,… literature, … biology and medicine and [religion] and geography and history and economics." And Merlin continues. At the end of his discourse Merlin says to the young and future King Arthur, "Do you think you have learned anything?" To which Arthur replies, "I have learned and been happy."

My hope for each graduate of the Wake Forest of our future is that he or she, if asked the question on Commencement Day, "Do you think you have learned anything?," will be able to say "I truly love what Wake Forest stands for. I have made friends, I have conducted myself with honor, I have learned, and I have been happy."

Edwin G. Wilson
Provost Emeritus
July 15, 2010
University Summer Leadership Conference

Afterword

GROWING UP ON FACULTY DRIVE across from the Wake Forest campus in the 1960s, I first knew Dr. Wilson as a friendly administrator and a faithful fan of the Wake Forest Demon Deacons. But my first experience of Dr. Wilson the Professor occurred when I enrolled in two of his famous courses, "British Romantic Poetry" and "Blake, Yeats, and Thomas." From the first moment he spoke aloud, I fell in love with William Wordsworth, and the abundant and profound poems of Coleridge, Keats, Byron, and Shelley that would figure in my own teaching career. Dr. Wilson's courses were usually scheduled for Friday afternoons. The jukeboxes blared from the fraternity houses, and dogs caught Frisbees. Sixty of us sat in Tribble Hall, mesmerized by his inspired readings of favorite lines, his lectures that taught us why we should study these poems and keep them in our hearts for the rest our lives.

As we arrived in class, Dr. Wilson was already writing passages of poetry on the board, along with numerous secondary sources that we felt compelled to pursue. Later, he would refer to these books with the enthusiasm of the gifted scholar he's always been. We wanted to memorize the poetry, check out the biographies and critical histories, and write a paper that was worthy of him. We felt honored to be in his presence, and his Wake Forest family still does, whenever we run into him in his black-and-gold library office, the Food Court, or the football stadium.

Dr. Wilson embodies all that is good and outstanding about our university. Known as "Mr. Wake Forest," he resembles our beloved mascot, with his handsome face, beautiful gray hair, and the fierce purpose that our athletic teams take to the field. As the bearer of Wake Forest's highest values, Dr. Wilson continues to espouse the importance of making our college accessible to the kind of young people who first benefited from Wake Forest's mission – North Carolina's poor, its ethnically diverse, its first generation of students who dream of being among "the finest" and "unrivalled by any."

Dr. Wilson was an undergraduate at the Old Campus, to which he returns once a year, as do the young and old to celebrate Wake Forest's beginnings at the Calvin Jones House, erected in 1834. After Dr. Wilson received his PhD from Harvard, he came back to North Carolina to teach at the New Campus in Winston-Salem, where he was subsequently appointed Dean, Provost, and he became a recipient of Wake Forest's highest honor, the Medallion of Merit.

Dr. Wilson has influenced generations of the Wake Forest community with his courage, faith, and vision. His belief in what Wake Forest can become reminds us of the importance of a liberal arts education and the sustaining power of the intellectual life.

It is fitting that he has published this book of eulogies that memorialize many of the faculty and staff who made the pilgrimage to Wake Forest, or joined its mission later in Winston-Salem. The souls he commemorates here in his eloquent reminiscenses serve as lasting memorials to the dedication of those who spent their professional lives making Wake Forest "Mother so Dear."

Catherine Burroughs

About the Author

EDWIN GRAVES WILSON is Professor Emeritus of English and Provost Emeritus of Wake Forest University. A native of Leaksville (now Eden), North Carolina, he entered Wake Forest College in 1939. Having earned his bachelor of arts degree summa cum laude in 1943, he served for three years as an officer in the United States Navy. He then enrolled in graduate school at Harvard University, where he was awarded the master of arts degree in 1948 and the doctor of philosophy degree in 1952.

He returned to his alma mater to teach and was named Professor of English in 1959. Generations of students enrolled in his courses in the British Romantic Poets and the poetry of Blake, Yeats, and Thomas.

In 1960, he was named Dean of the College by President Harold Tribble and was appointed Provost in 1967 by President James Ralph Scales, a position he held for 23 years. He later served in the administration of President Thomas K. Hearn, Jr. as Senior Vice President and in the administration of President Nathan O. Hatch as Provost Emeritus.

Mr. Wilson is the recipient of the Reinhardt Award for Distinguished Teaching; the Distinguished Alumni Citation; and Wake Forest's highest award for service, the Medallion of Merit. He served the city of Winston-Salem and the state of North Carolina in many capacities, including the presidencies of the Winston-Salem Arts Council, the Piedmont Opera Theatre, the North Carolina Association of Colleges and Universities, and the Rotary Club. He has also been a member of the North Carolina Humanities Council and the North Carolina Arts Council and received the North Carolina Award for Public Service. In 2014 he was awarded the John Tyler Caldwell Award for the Humanities by the NC Humanities Council and in 2017 he was inducted into the Wake Forest Sports Hall of Fame, having served as a past president of the Atlantic Coast Conference.

Mr. Wilson is married to the poet and author Emily Herring Wilson. They are the parents of three children and have four grandchildren.

About the Editors

CATHERINE BURROUGHS, a graduate of Wake Forest University in 1980, is Courtesy Lecturer of English and the Performing Arts and Media Studies departments at Cornell University, as well as a member of Actors' Equity Association. Throughout her career, she has focused on the contributions to theatre and playwrighting of women writers between 1750 and 1830. Her book, *Closet Stages: Joanna Baillie and the Theater Theory of British Romantic Women Writers* (University of Pennsylvania Press, 1997), helped to make Baillie canonical and encouraged scholarship on theatre theorists of the Romantic period and the broader topic of gender and the stage. In addition to many articles on British Romantic theatre and drama, her publications include: *Reading the Social Body* (Co-Ed., University of Iowa Press, 1993); *Women in British Romantic Theatre: Drama, Performance, and Society, 1790 – 1840* (Ed., Cambridge University Press, 2000; re-printed in Paper 2006); *Approaches to Teaching Early British Women Playwrights* (Modern Language Association, 2010); *Closet Drama: History, Theory, Form* (Routledge, 2019); and *Women's Theatre Theory and Dramatic Criticism: An Anthology.* (Co-Ed. J. Ellen Gainor. Routledge, Forthcoming). Catherine lives on Edisto Island in South Carolina with her husband, Rick Bogel, and they have a son, Nicholas Bogel-Burroughs.

TAMARA MCLAUGHLIN majored in English and graduated from Wake Forest in 1999. Her work has been varied – teaching English overseas, spending a decade in advertising and marketing, and then moving into non-profit management where she served as the Executive Director for Donate Life North Carolina. She returned to her alma mater to work for Dr. Wilson in 2014, resuming a long-standing friendship that began while he was her undergraduate advisor and she worked for him as a student. Currently, she is the Business and Communications Manager for the Wellbeing Collaborative at Wake Forest, a national initiative to assess and improve wellbeing in higher education. A strong believer in public education, her volunteer efforts have included a variety of PTA roles in local schools. An avid horseback rider, she also volunteers with Riverwood's equine assisted learning programs. She and her husband Chris McLaughlin (BA '99, MBA '04) live in Winston Salem with their two children, Connor and Payden.